Classic
ITALIAN
COOKING

Classic
ITALIAN
COOKING
Recipes for mastering the Italian kitchen

VALENTINA HARRIS

MQP

For Jamie and Ben - with eternal love

An Hachette Livre Company
First published in Great Britain in 2005 by MQ Publications,
a division of Octopus Publishing Group Ltd
2–4 Heron Quays, London E14 4JP
www.octopusbooks.co.uk

ISBN: 978-1-84072-956-6

10 9 8 7 6 5 4 3

Printed and bound in China

This book contains the opinions and ideas of the author. It is intended to provide helpful and
informative material on the subjects addressed in this book and is sold with the understanding
that the author and publisher are not engaged in rendering any kind of personal professional
services in this book. The author and publisher disclaim all responsibility for any liability, loss
or risk, personal or otherwise, which is incurred as a consequence, directly or indirectly, of the
use and application of any of the contents of this book.

contents

introduction

From a very early age, I understood the basic principles of Italian food. That it should respect the seasons in terms of the ingredients used, that food should be sourced as locally as possible, and that ultimately the less you mess around with it all the better! I grew up celebrating the great love affair of my parents in a huge house in Tuscany filled with friends and family. Everything seemed to circulate around the activities of the dining room and kitchen. As a little girl and the youngest of a large brood, I would gravitate towards the kitchen, where my mother was often found discussing menus and recipes with various other members of the household. Over intense conversations about the quality of ingredients or the quantities required for the next lunch or dinner, the seeds of my growing passion for cooking and for food were deeply sown. And my understanding of the subtleties, which underlie something so apparently simple, was possibly the most valuable lesson of all.

When the house was first given to my parents as a wedding gift by my grandfather in the late 1940s, it was a wreck. Living among the ruins of this great, happy house were various individuals who had ended up homeless and

displaced as a result of the war. The house, although bombed beyond recognition, still had a clean water well, a working fireplace, and offered a certain degree of shelter. One of those biding his time was a young man who had been a chef in a famous Milanese restaurant before the war. My parents, in a flash of brilliance, kept him on and he became much more than our cook. Beppino developed our vines, kept chickens, pigs, and rabbits for the table, established a wonderfully lush vegetable garden, several fruit trees, and rebuilt the house with the help of other local craftsmen.

Growing up with Beppino around me meant that I learned the most fundamental aspect of food preparation. He taught me the most basic principle—where the food actually comes from in the first place. Long, long before organic food became fashionable, Beppino would lecture me on the evils of pesticides, additives, and artificial fertilizers. I absorbed his words like a sponge, always secure in the absolute knowledge that his food always tasted better than anything I was ever likely to eat anywhere, and that somehow the two were linked. It still does, many years on, when I return to cook and eat with him from time to time and we reminisce, always about food we have eaten and cooked together.

His repertoire was always linked to the seasonal availability of the ingredients. As soon as the first whiff of fall was in the air, with bonfires smoldering in the dampness, he would set off on his bicycle for the nearest corn mill where the new season polenta flour would be freshly ground. Pedaling frantically behind him on my own bicycle, I would then kneel beside him and let the bright yellow flour run through my fingers as he explained to me why this would taste so much better than the polenta flour that had dried out and lost its natural moisture.

A few hours later, after much arm straining stirring, the proof would be there on the plate—a huge slab of fragrant polenta, with some amazing stew piled over and beside it. As we tucked in, Beppino would look at me gravely and explain how polenta is actually not as nutritious as I might imagine, "you're hungry again all too soon," he'd say "there is little or no substance to it, it doesn't have what it takes, not really." Much later I read about how people in northern Italy, before, during, and after the Second World War, suffered terribly from malnutrition as a result of their basic polenta diet, and I learned that the tiny stature of so many older Italians living in those areas where polenta was the only real staple was not merely coincidental. Beppino came from the Vicenza area of the Veneto. His mother, who throughout her 96 years must have eaten polenta in some form almost daily, was the tiniest, scrawniest looking woman—just like countless others of her generation.

By the time I was eight years old I had opened my first restaurant—in the sandbox in the garden of our house. I only served sand pies and various leaves and flowers, but I did it all properly, with borrowed tablecloths, china, sparkling glasses, and cutlery, presenting each and every member of the household who was kind enough to indulge me with a handwritten bill at the end! A year or so later I began to spend every lira of my pocket money on real ingredients and my parents bought me several small camping stoves, something that would be gravely frowned upon in this day and age! But finally I was able to cook for my customers and the die was cast as far as my destiny was concerned.

Much later, I made the decision to go to chef school in Rome and was fortunate enough to be taught by one of Italy's greatest master chefs, a man called Carnacina. Although very old at the time, he was another mine of information and taught me so much about the principles of classical Italian cuisine. It was around this time that the concept of there being no such thing as Italian food as such began to take shape for me.

To understand this principle you have to go a little way back into history. The unification of Italy took place about 150 years ago, in the 1860s. Prior to this, the country was a collection of papal states, foreign states, principalities, and dukedoms, with constant fighting and ever changing boundary lines. Since the unification, and the creation of the Italy we know and love so much now, 20 separate regions have been created. Each one of these 20 regions carries some vestige of its past, something which history has left behind in terms of the local dialect, the art and architecture, music, and so on. To my mind, it is also the food, the ingredients, and the cooking methods of each region that reflect certain aspects of the history of that area with a clarity that is impossible to ignore. It is this, added to the geography and climate, that gives each region of Italy its own culinary identity, which gives us not one but 20 different cuisines to choose from, through which it is possible, in many cases, to make a direct link to the regions' pasts. It is out of these 20 regional cuisines that the great classic dishes of Italy are derived.

In the north, for example, there is more rain, given the mountainous terrain, than in the south. This results in their being sufficient fodder to support both dairy cattle and beef cattle—resulting in most of the best loved Italian cheeses being produced here, as well as many veal and beef recipes. To the west, the recipes are reminiscent of the region's historical links with the southeastern corner of France, while to the far east, the influence of the Austro Hungarian Empire is still there to taste quite plainly in the choice of local ingredients which include such things as horseradish, paprika, beer, and beet, to name but a few.

All over the north, in the marshy flat plains between Lombardy and Piedmont and in the Po delta are the paddy fields. They have expanded since the time of my ancestor Francesco Sforza Duke of Milan, who was responsible for overseeing the intricate drainage system that exists on the plain, using the Alpine snow melt to create the right conditions for growing this valuable crop. This is the rice used to make Italy's great rice dish—risotto, which along with cornmeal to make polenta, form the starch basis of the traditional diet of the northern areas, with butter or lard being the choice for cooking fats. Olive trees cannot survive the cold northern winters in order to yield a crop for olive oil.

Traveling further south into the central area of Italy, comprising, by and large, Emilia Romagna, Tuscany, the Marche, Lazio, and Umbria, fresh pasta made with eggs and flour replaces the starch staples of risotto and polenta, alongside legumes, thick soups, and roasted meats.

Still further south, the now famously healthy Mediterranean diet is standard fare. Fresh pasta is replaced by dried durum wheat pasta and bread as staple starches, and then olive oil, olives, tomatoes, salted anchovies, capers, dried chiles, garlic bread, very little meat or animal fats to speak of, but fish and seafood for protein and luscious vegetables for flavor and color.

Within these three basic areas of Italy, each and every region has its own culinary identity, recipes, and culinary traditions that link the history of the region to the food on the plate. They say: *dimmi cosa mangi e ti diro di dove sei*—tell me what you eat and I'll know where you're from. The food of Italy is so varied that you can eat a selection of local dishes in one part of this amazing, small country, jump on a train and be in a different part of the country within hours, eating a completely different range of dishes. No other country can boast such differences and it is a very clear testament of how rich the gastronomy of Italy really is.

Naturally, the unstoppable march of progress means that traveling and the exchange of everything, including traditional regional recipes, within Italy is getting ever quicker and easier. Be it by autostrada, the railway system, or via an internal flight. The boundaries between one region and another are becoming more blurred all the time, and it becomes more difficult, with the passage of time, to distinguish one region's traditional culinary customs from another. Yet the differences are all still very clearly visible. This enormous collection of regional recipes, for good or for bad, must be considered to be classical Italian cuisine.

To find the purest Italian regional cuisine, one must look to Tuscany. This region is the only one in the whole of the country that has never been invaded or ruled by a foreign power, and as such it is generally considered to be the most authentically Italian region of the country. The Italian spoken in Tuscany is also considered to be the purest Italian language. Tuscany's culinary repertoire contains many of the most important great classic dishes, based mostly around thick, rich bean soups, plenty of roasted meats, and the all pervading scent of rosemary, not forgetting the rich sweetmeats and pastries of cities such as Siena.

I admit to being a bit of a purist when it comes to Italian food. I believe that it is important to uphold the culinary customs and traditions of this beautiful country, lest we should lose an essential part of the country's cultural background. While I am the first to applaud the ever-changing evolution of food and understand that it is important to experiment with flavors and textures, I still firmly uphold the principles of traditional Italian dishes. How could it be any other way for me, after the training I received at such a very early age? So here is this collection of recipes containing the best of Italy's classic recipes, all of which have lasted the test of time and are just as wonderful today as they were when they were first created. But eating is believing!

Buon Appetito.

Valentina Harris

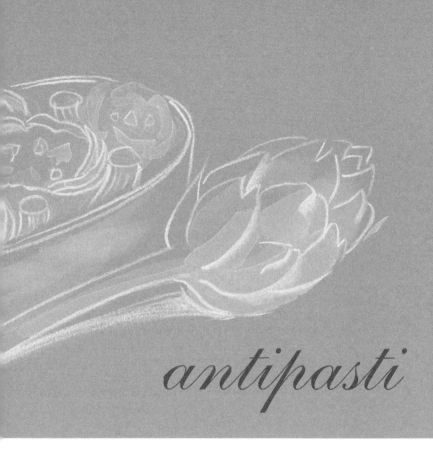

antipasti

antipasto di coniglio

RABBIT ANTIPASTO

This is a real classic from Piemonte, a long, slow recipe, it takes about three days to prepare! It is absolutely delicious served with sweet roasted peppers or porcini mushrooms preserved in olive oil.

Serves 6

2 carrots
2 celery stalks
1 onion, peeled
1 fresh rosemary sprig
½ rabbit, jointed
2 garlic cloves, sliced thinly
7 bay leaves
8 juniper berries
10 black peppercorns
sea salt
extra virgin olive oil

1 Place the carrots, celery, onion, and rosemary in a large heavy saucepan, cover with water, and bring to a boil.

2 When the water boils, add the rabbit and return to the boil. Reduce the heat and simmer gently for about 30 minutes. Turn off the heat and allow the rabbit to cool down completely in the broth.

3 When the rabbit is cold, take all the meat off the bones. Place a layer of meat in the base of a pudding bowl or loaf pan or shaped terrine mould, cover with a layer of sliced garlic, bay leaves, juniper berries, peppercorns, and salt. Repeat until all the ingredients have been used up.

4 Cover generously with olive oil and store in the refrigerator for 2 to 3 days.

5 Serve on a platter, removing the garlic slices, peppercorns, and bay leaves.

NOTE ~ Both wild and domestic rabbits are available. The main difference being that the former has darker flesh and a more distinctive flavor of game.

insalata di frutti di mare

SEAFOOD SALAD

The shellfish and crustacea for this delicious salad can vary according to availability, as long as whatever you use is perfectly fresh and sweet to the taste. The key is that when choosing your ingredients, nothing should smell unpleasant or fishy, retaining instead the fresh perfume of the seashore. Baby clams (vongole) can be muddy, especially if not fished from sandy shores, so be sure to leave them in a bowl of cold water for a few hours before rinsing thoroughly and steaming.

Serves 4

6oz fresh squid, cleaned and cut into neat strips and rings
2¼lb fresh mussels, scrubbed and cleaned
2¼lb fresh baby clams (vongole), scrubbed and cleaned
6oz fresh shrimp (small)
4 jumbo fresh shrimp
juice of half lemon
6 tablespoons extra virgin olive oil
3 tablespoons chopped fresh Italian parsley
sea salt and freshly ground black pepper

TO SERVE
lemon slices

1 Place the squid in a saucepan of salted water and boil for 25 to 30 minutes, or until tender. Discard any mussel or clam shells that are closed. Place the mussels and clams in a separate large saucepan with a little water, cover, and steam for about 8 minutes. When all the shells have opened, drain and discard any that remain closed.

2 Wash the small and jumbo shrimp carefully. Place the small shrimp in a saucepan and cover with cold water. Bring to a boil and cook for 1 minute. Drain and allow to cool before removing the shells.

3 Place the jumbo shrimp in a separate saucepan and cover with cold water. Bring to a boil and cook for 2 minutes. Drain and allow to cool until required.

4 Remove the mussels from their shells and put them in a bowl with the small shrimp and squid. Mix them all together, then add the lemon juice, olive oil, parsley, and pepper to taste. Mix again, then season with salt.

5 Serve the seafood salad at room temperature garnished with the 4 jumbo shrimp and lemon slices.

caponata

WARM EGGPLANT AND OLIVE SALAD

A very traditional antipasto from Sicily and the deep south of Italy. I like to serve it alongside other dishes, particularly soft pecorino cheeses, ricotta, or a bowl of fresh shrimp cooked in their shells. Many versions of this dish still exist, but I especially like this one as it is simple, but has an interesting selection of ingredients and textures.

∽

Serves 6

9 cups cubed eggplants
sea salt
½ cup olive oil
⅓ cup chopped onion
¾ cup assorted Italian pickles (a combination of onions, sweet peppers, cauliflowers, cocktail pickles)
2 tablespoons capers, rinsed and dried
6 celery leaves, chopped
⅛ cup green olives, stoned
1 tablespoon granulated sugar
½ cup red wine vinegar
2 tablespoons pine nuts

1 Sprinkle the cubed eggplants with salt, and place them in a colander. Cover the colander with a plate and then a weight over the top and stand it in the sink for about 1 hour or longer if possible to let the bitter juices of the eggplants drain away. Rinse under cold running water and dry them thoroughly.

2 Divide the olive oil between two deep skillets. Add the dried eggplant cubes to one pan and fry until the eggplants are soft and well browned. Remove them from the oil and leave them to drain on paper towels.

3 Add the onion, pickles, capers, celery leaves, and olives to the other skillet and fry over a low heat for about 15 minutes.

4 Add the sugar and vinegar to the onion mixture, let the acidic fumes of the vinegar evaporate, then stir in the eggplant and the pine nuts.

5 Serve as part of an antipasto course, either spooned over toasted crusty bread, or as an accompaniment to cured meat or many simple fish or shellfish dishes.

NOTE ~ Although this dish is best served warm, it is also very good served cold, especially alongside cold meats.

carpaccio di carciofi

RAW ARTICHOKE SALAD

The original carpaccio was made in Venice at the original Cipriani bar in Piazza San Marco, at the special request of a regular customer. It consisted of very finely sliced veal, dressed with lemon juice, olive oil, and salt and pepper, then finished with a scattering of shaved Parmigiano Reggiano. The name carpaccio has since come to be given to all kinds of dishes where the main ingredient, from swordfish to pineapples and beyond, has been sliced thin. Here is how to make a carpaccio out of the tender hearts of fresh artichokes, mushrooms, or zucchini.

❧

Serves 4

1 lemon, halved
8 large artichokes
a large handful of fresh flat-leaf parsley, chopped fine
6oz Parmigiano Reggiano shavings
juice of ½ lemon
extra virgin olive oil
salt and freshly ground black pepper

1 Fill a bowl large enough to hold the prepared artichokes with cold water and squeeze the juice of one lemon half into it. Place the lemon halves into the water.

2 Prepare the artichokes by trimming the stalk and peeling away the tough outer leaves. Cut off the tops and remove the chokes by scooping them out with a teaspoon. Place the tender hearts into the bowl of cold water—this helps to prevent the artichokes from blackening.

3 Drain the artichokes carefully, dry thoroughly, and then slice them as thin as possible.

4 Arrange them flat on a large platter, scatter with the chopped parsley and Parmigiano Reggiano shavings.

5 Sprinkle with lemon juice, olive oil, and seasoning and serve. Serve within 30 minutes.

NOTE ~ This recipe can also be made using tender young zucchini or large, tasty mushrooms, sliced very thin. You can also substitute mint or another fresh herb of your choice for the parsley if desired.

peperoni arrosto in insalata

ROASTED SWEET PEPPER SALAD

This is such a classic dish. It is delicious, though perhaps a little heavy compared to many other possible antipasti. This is due to the raw garlic and the nature of the peppers—but it is incredibly tasty. In most cases, people find the external papery skin of the pepper hard to digest, and once this is removed, suffer no ill effects. Whatever the facts, in Italian kitchen lore anything with peppers is considered to be pesante— heavy on the digestion!

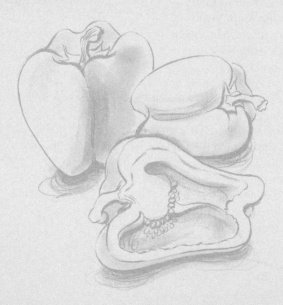

6 large red and/or yellow bell peppers
3 garlic cloves, chopped
a large handful of fresh Italian parsley, roughly chopped
8 tablespoons extra virgin olive oil
sea salt and freshly ground black pepper

1 Preheat the oven to 400°F. Wash the peppers, arrange them either directly on a grill rack in the oven or in a baking tray and roast for about 30 minutes, or until browned and soft.

2 Remove them from the oven and lay them in a deep tray on the countertop. Invert a large glass or china bowl over the peppers to cover them so that they can steam as they cool, thus loosening their skins.

3 As soon as the peppers are cool enough to handle easily, slip off their thin, papery skins and remove the seeds.

4 Arrange the prepared peppers in thick slices, slightly overlapping, on a platter or in a shallow-sided bowl.

5 Scatter the garlic and parsley over the peppers and sprinkle with the olive oil and salt and pepper. Mix briefly, then allow to stand for at least 1 hour to allow the flavors to develop before serving.

pomodori al forno ripieni di riso

BAKED STUFFED TOMATOES WITH RICE

I remember, as a little girl, becoming intoxicated by the unique perfume of ripe tomatoes, deliberately bruising the leaves as I passed by to get another burst, then picking them and watching them go from my basket to the roasting pan in a matter of minutes. They would emerge after one short hour simply bursting at the seams with nutty rice, the tomato sweetened to a dense, burnt caramel by the heat of the oven mixed with the magic of olive oil. The potato slices and wedges, though delicious, are really only there to keep the tomatoes upright, so use them as you see fit to wedge the tomatoes firmly.

Serves 6

12 fist-sized ripe, firm tomatoes
½ cup long-grain rice
2 garlic cloves, chopped fine
5 tablespoons olive oil
10 fresh basil leaves, torn into shreds
1 tablespoon dried oregano
1 large potato, cut into slices and wedges as required
salt and freshly ground black pepper

1 Preheat the oven to 350°C. Slice the tops off the tomatoes and set them aside. Using a teaspoon scoop out the inside of the tomatoes and discard the seeds. Chop the flesh of the tomatoes and put it into a bowl.

2 Add the rice and garlic, half the olive oil, and the herbs. Season well with salt and pepper and use to fill all the tomatoes. Replace the lids on the tomatoes.

3 Grease an ovenproof dish lightly with most of the remaining olive oil and lay the potato slices on the base.

4 Place each tomato on a slice of raw potato, then pour a little cold water around the tomatoes and potato.

5 Pour the last of the olive oil on top of the tomatoes and bake in the oven for about 55 minutes, or until the rice is tender and the tomatoes are soft. You may need to add more water during cooking if the tomatoes have dried out too much. Serve warm or cold.

sardine impanate

FRIED SARDINES WITH A CRISP BREAD CRUMB COATING

These always remind me of going to exhibitions in Venice, where trays piled high with these delicious fish are passed around the room and are washed down with plenty of ice cold Prosecco. The fish must be incredibly fresh and properly gutted and boned before using. In particular, any pieces of the fish gut, however small, will leave a bitter taste through the whole dish. Be sure to rinse and dry all the fish with care.

Serves 6

2¼lb fresh sardines or large anchovies
3 eggs, thoroughly beaten
sunflower oil for deep-frying
10 tablespoons very fine dried white bread crumbs
sea salt and freshly ground black pepper

TO SERVE
lemon wedges

1 Remove the head from each fish, pulling downward to remove the backbone at the same time.

2 Wash the inside and the outside of the fish thoroughly under cold running water. You should end up with a flat, headless, filleted, but whole fish. Leave the fish to drain in a colander and continue with all the other fish.

3 Place all the cleaned, filleted fish into a large bowl with the beaten eggs and, using your hands, mix gently until the fish are thoroughly coated in the egg. Allow to stand in the refrigerator for about 1 hour.

4 Heat the sunflower oil gently in a wide, deep skillet. While it heats, spread the bread crumbs out on a plate. Take the fish out of the egg, draining off any excess, then coat generously and thoroughly in the bread crumbs.

5 Using the heel of your hand, press the breaded fish down thoroughly on a board, making sure the fish is completely coated in bread crumbs. Shake to remove any excess crumbs.

6 Fry for 2 or 3 minutes in the sizzling hot oil, drain thoroughly on clean dry paper towels, and serve hot, sprinkled with a little salt and pepper, and accompanied by a wedge of lemon.

The antipasti course is supposed to liven up the taste buds and get the gastric juices flowing in anticipation of what is to follow. Ideally, it should not be too filling and be made up of dishes such as salads, paper thin slices of cured meats, and very simply prepared, light morsels of dishes based around meat, fish, seafood, cheese, vegetables, and fruit. Antipasti can be hot or cold, at room temperature, or chilled. They can be elaborate or incredibly simple. The word itself means before the meal and as such needs to be as light as possible.

Cured meats are often a part of antipasti, and of these cured ham or prosciutto crudo is one of the most popular, along with Italy's vast range of different kinds of salami.

Prosciutto crudo is the most noble of all the Italian cured meats with a tradition that can be traced back to the times of ancient Rome. It is made from the most highly selected hindquarters of pork. The curing process is very simple. Apart from the excellent meat itself, the only other ingredient used is salt, which is massaged into the meat. After a period of rest, the meat is washed carefully in warm water, then allowed to dry and cure over a long period of time. During this curing process the meat takes on the characteristics of flavor and texture that have made it so famous worldwide. There are several different kinds of Italian *prosciutto crudo*. The best known are *prosciutto di Parma* and *prosciutto di San Daniele*, but there are many others which are also superb. These include Toscano, Veneto Berico-Euganeo, Norcia, Modena, and Jambon de Bosses.

Salami is one of the most ancient of cured meats. It has very old traditions that have evolved over the centuries, with many distinct regional specialties. These different regional specialties can be identified by the way in which the meat has been ground—fine, medium or coarse—and by the addition of other flavorings such as garlic, chile, fennel seeds, or wine. Generally speaking, salami has a long, rounded sausage shape and is available in many different sizes according to type. Once sliced, it should be reddish in color with well-defined white fatty spots. The ingredients used in the curing process obviously have an effect on the end flavor, which means that there are enormous variations depending upon where the salami was made. Different tastes range from the classical savory intensity through to those that are spicy or smoked after curing.

The only Italian cured meat that is not made from pork is the delicious Bresaola from the region of Lombardy. Made from specially selected beef haunches, this meat is enjoyed all over the country. The beef is seasoned with a special mixture of salt, pepper, and other spices and cured in controlled humidity and temperature. The finished product is then placed inside pork gut casings and cured for a further period of between one and three months. The end result is a cured meat that is characteristically intense and uniformly red in color with a delicate, slightly salty aroma.

It is traditionally served sliced paper thin, with a dressing of olive oil, lemon juice, and pepper, accompanied by some good bread.

soups

minestra di pasta e ceci

SOUP WITH PASTA AND CHICKPEAS

This is one of the oldest (some say Ancient Roman) soup recipes, still cooked and served like this in many a downtown Roman trattoria! If you find the anchovy and/or chile not to your taste, simply leave them out altogether. You can also use dried chickpeas as an alternative, but they will need to soak for a long time in several changes of cold, fresh water to avoid fermentation. When I use dried chickpeas I soak them for about 24 hours and change the water four or five times.

Serves 6

2½ cups canned chickpeas
1 small branch fresh rosemary
5 tablespoons extra virgin olive oil
2 large garlic cloves, chopped
½ dried red chile, chopped
3 canned anchovy fillets, drained, rinsed, drained, and chopped
1 tablespoon tomato paste
1 cup cold water
3 cups small tubular pasta suitable for soups
salt and freshly ground black pepper

1 Rinse the chickpeas, then place in a large saucepan. Cover generously with fresh cold water, add the rosemary, and bring to a boil. Reduce the heat and simmer until very soft, about 30 minutes to 1 hour.

2 Meanwhile, heat the olive oil in another similar-size saucepan. Add the garlic, chile and chopped anchovies and fry briefly over a medium to low heat until the anchovies have begun to melt.

3 Stir in the tomato paste and add the water. Stir and allow to simmer for about 20 minutes.

4 Add the cooked chickpeas with their cooking liquid and return to a boil. Stir in the pasta and cook for about 10 minutes, or until soft. Season with a little salt and a generous amount of pepper. Serve immediately.

minestra di zucchine

ZUCCHINI SOUP

This is one of my favorite family recipes. It was one of the many ways we used the endless supply of zucchini that seemed to spring up in the vegetable garden overnight! This soup is really easy to make and can be finished with a generous grating of Parmigiano Reggiano or a handful of chopped fresh herbs. Use really fresh, firm zucchini that have not begun to lose their luster or firmness.

Serves 4

6 medium-size zucchini
1 tablespoon butter or vegetable oil
1 onion, sliced
1 carrot, chopped fine
1 celery stalk, chopped
1 garlic clove, crushed
6 cups vegetable or chicken broth
sea salt and freshly ground pepper

TO SERVE
freshly grated Parmigiano Reggiano or chopped fresh herbs

1 Wash and dry the zucchini. Five of them can be chopped roughly, but the sixth needs to be grated and left to drain through a fine strainer until required. This is because it might expunge quite a lot of watery, tasteless fluid that you won't want in your soup.

2 Heat the butter or oil gently in a large saucepan. Add the onion, carrot, celery, and garlic. Add the chopped zucchini and stir together. Half cover the saucepan with a lid and allow the vegetables to sweat for about 5 minutes, shaking the saucepan several times.

3 When the vegetables are reasonably soft, add the broth and simmer for about 10 minutes until the vegetables begin to fall apart. Taste and adjust the seasoning if necessary.

4 Push through a food mill or purée with a hand-held blender, then stir in the raw grated zucchini.

5 Serve with grated Parmigiano Reggiano or chopped fresh herbs, or both.

minestrone

BIG VEGETABLE SOUP WITH BEANS AND PASTA OR RICE

The great classic Italian soup! It means "big soup" in the sense that it is designed to fill you up and make you feel fully satisfied. It differs from, and should not be confused with, the other great classic: Pasta e Fagioli *(see page 48), a version of which appears, with only slight variations, in almost every region of Italy. Minestrone, on the other hand, is originally a soup from Lombardy.*

Serves 6

1 cup fresh, dried or canned cranberry beans
4 tablespoons olive oil
1 onion, chopped fine
a handful of fresh Italian parsley, chopped
4 cups chopped green leaf vegetables, such as spinach, cabbage, Swiss chard, lettuce leaves, turnip tops
2 zucchini, cubed
1 potato, peeled and cubed
1 carrot, cubed
1 cup short stubby pasta or long-grain rice
salt and freshly ground black pepper

TO SERVE
olive oil
freshly grated Parmigiano Reggiano

1 If using dried or fresh beans, soak them overnight in cold water, then drain and rinse. Boil quickly in salted water for 5 minutes to remove the natural toxins, then drain and rinse again. Cover the beans generously with cold water and simmer gently for about 40 minutes, or until tender. Do not add salt to the water until the beans are tender because this will cause the skin to shrivel and harden.

2 If using canned beans, drain and rinse carefully before adding to the soup.

3 Heat the olive oil in a large, heavy saucepan. Add the onion and fry for about 5 minutes. Add the parsley and all the vegetables, then stir and cook for a further 5 minutes.

4 Pour in the beans and all their water. Add more water if necessary to maintain enough liquid to cook the vegetables. Simmer gently for about 60 minutes, stirring frequently and topping up with liquid whenever necessary.

5 Once the vegetables are thoroughly cooked, add the pasta or rice and cook until the pasta or rice are tender. Season with salt and pepper to taste.

6 Serve hot with olive oil and grated Parmigiano Reggiano. Alternatively, allow to cool and serve at room temperature or even chilled.

NOTE ~ **Please note that the soup will thicken considerably as it cools down. In summer, it is nice to serve Minestrone tepid, with a spoonful of pesto stirred through at the last moment.**

pappa al pomodoro

TOMATO AND BREAD SOUP

This is a very thick soup, which makes the best of the glut of over-ripe tomatoes at the end of a Tuscan summer, combined with that ever present stand-by ingredient, stale bread. It is marvelous served lukewarm with plenty of basil and extra olive oil to drizzle over it. Oddly, this soup was made famous during the sixties because there was a pop song, sung by Rita Pavone, which was all about how wonderful this soup was ... I think, though the soup could well have been symbolic of something quite different! It is a very traditional part of the classic Tuscan menu repertoire.

Serves 6

6 cups vegetable, chicken or meat broth
1 large onion, chopped
2¾lb very ripe, soft tomatoes, roughly chopped
8 tablespoons olive oil
**14oz stale crusty Italian bread, crusts removed and
sliced thin**
3 garlic cloves, crushed
a handful of fresh basil leaves, chopped
sea salt and freshly ground black pepper

1 Heat the broth gently in a large saucepan. While it is warming, heat the olive oil in a separate saucepan and fry the onion and tomatoes together over a low heat for about 10 minutes or until softened.

2 Push the onion and tomato mixture through a food mill or strainer and add it to the hot broth. Stir thoroughly.

3 Add the bread, garlic, and basil and season with salt and pepper to taste. Cover and simmer gently for about 45 minutes or until thick and creamy, stirring occasionally.

4 Stir in the remaining oil, taste and adjust the seasoning if necessary, add some more basil and serve either hot or at room temperature.

SERVING SUGGESTION ~ Serve this delicious soup with a traditional Italian bread, such as Pugliese bread.

passato di verdura

VEGETABLE SOUP

A typical country summertime soup, prepared when all the vegetables are at their peak of luscious ripeness. When I was growing up in Tuscany we would eat this soup about once a week, usually made with the vegetables grown in our own garden. The trick is to subtly blend all the vegetable flavors together so you end up being able to taste the vegetables as an amalgamation as well as separately.

It is delicious served with lightly oiled croûtons made from coarse, crusty bread, although you can also add a tiny handful of soup pasta or rice to make the soup more substantial. Freshly grated Parmigiano Reggiano is usually offered separately.

Serves 4

2 tablespoons olive oil
1 large onion, chopped
2 carrots, chopped
2 large celery stalks, chopped
1 large zucchini or 2 smaller ones, peeled
1 large potato, peeled
1 large, very ripe tomato, peeled
a large handful of green beans, trimmed
a large handful of fresh spinach leaves
a small handful of fresh Italian parsley
a small handful of fresh basil
sea salt and freshly ground black pepper

1 Heat the olive oil in a saucepan over a low heat. Add the onion, carrots, and celery and fry for until softened.

2 Cut the zucchini, potato, tomato, and beans into cubes and add them to the pan. Stir and cook for about 5 minutes, moistening with a little water if necessary.

3 Add the spinach leaves to the pan. Chop the herbs and stir them through. Cover generously with cold water and bring to a low simmer. Leave to cook gently for about 40 minutes, stirring occasionally. Taste and adjust seasoning and remove from the heat.

4 Allow to stand until cool, then push through a food mill or a strainer. Alternatively, process in a food processor until almost smooth. Return the soup to the saucepan and reheat until piping hot. Serve immediately.

pasta e fagioli

PASTA AND BEAN SOUP

There are so many recipes for this soup as every region of Italy seems to have their own version. Basically, the recipe is nearly always the same, with just a few variations such as the addition of tomato paste, herbs, pancetta, chile or sometimes a different kind of bean. Pasta does not feature traditionally in Venetian cuisine, so this is something of an exception to the rule.

Serves 4

1 cup dried, fresh or canned cannellini beans
2 tablespoons olive oil
3oz fatty pancetta or prosciutto, cubed
3 tablespoons olive oil
1 onion, chopped
1 carrot, chopped
1 celery stalk, chopped
4 cups good meat broth
1½ cups small soup pasta
sea salt and freshly ground black pepper

1 If using dried or fresh beans, soak overnight in cold water, then drain and rinse. Boil quickly in salted water for 5 minutes to remove the natural toxins, then drain and rinse again. Cover generously with fresh water and simmer gently for about 40 minutes, or until tender. If using canned beans, drain and set aside.

2 Heat the olive oil in a large saucepan. Add the pancetta or prosciutto, onion, carrot, and celery and fry until all the vegetables are soft.

3 Add the beans and stir well. Add the broth and simmer slowly until the beans are almost falling apart, about 30 minutes. Add the pasta and cook until the pasta is tender. Season with salt and pepper to taste and serve warm.

la stracciatella alla romana

ROMAN EGG AND CHEESE SOUP

This has always been considered to be a good soup for anybody whose appetite is failing due to illness. Very digestible, it is a nourishing, light soup to satisfy and comfort. The important ingredients are the chicken broth, which has to be good enough to enjoy on its own, and the absolute freshness of the eggs. Don't overdo the nutmeg or lemon peel, otherwise there is a risk of overpowering the other flavors in the soup.

Serves 4 to 6

6 eggs
6 heaping tablespoons freshly grated Parmigiano Reggiano
grated nutmeg or grated lemon peel to taste
6 cups rich, clear chicken broth
sea salt and freshly ground black pepper
a little finely chopped fresh Italian parsley, to garnish

1 Break the eggs into a large bowl and, using a whisk, beat until blended. Add the cheese and salt and pepper to taste.

2 Add either the nutmeg or lemon peel according to personal preference.

3 About 10 minutes before you wish to serve this delicate, light, and nourishing soup, bring the broth to a boil.

4 As soon as it is boiling, remove from the heat and pour in the egg mixture. Beat energetically to prevent lumps from forming for about 3 minutes or as soon as the eggs have cooked just enough to hold their raggedy shape, floating in the broth.

5 Ladle the soup into soup bowls and serve immediately sprinkled with a little fresh chopped parsley.

NOTE ~ The flavoring added to this soup varies slightly according to the region—in some areas nutmeg is added, while other regional cooks seem to prefer adding a little finely grated lemon peel.

salads

insalata di mortadella, funghi e parmigiano

SALAD OF MORTADELLA, MUSHROOMS, AND PARMIGIANO

This is a simple, clean-tasting salad, which is perfect to serve as a light appetizer. I discovered this salad in the city of Bologna, where most of the traditional dishes tend to be quite rich and heavy. I like to make the salad in a shallow bowl, though you may prefer to assemble it on separate plates. Try to use mushrooms that do not have a very strong taste, such as oyster mushrooms or brown caps. Mortadella, a lightly smoked Italian sausage, is a classic Italian ingredient and is usually used either as part of a sandwich or in salads like this one.

Serves 4

10oz mushrooms of your choice, cleaned and sliced thin
6oz mortadella, sliced and cut into long sticks
juice of ½ lemon
1 tablespoon chopped fresh mint
4 tablespoons chopped fresh Italian parsley
about 4 tablespoons extra virgin olive oil
4oz Parmigiano Reggiano shavings
sea salt and freshly ground black pepper

1 For a more elegant and formal occasion, arrange the mushrooms in a single layer on an attractive serving plate and cover with a layer of mortadella.

2 Mix the lemon juice, mint, and parsley together in a small bowl and add salt and pepper to taste.

3 Add the olive oil and beat thoroughly until the oil thickens. Taste and adjust the seasoning if necessary, then drizzle the dressing over the salad and sprinkle with the Parmigiano Reggiano shavings.

4 Alternatively, place the mushrooms, mortadella, and the Parmigiano Reggiano in a shallow bowl and mix together. Pour the dressing over the salad, mix thoroughly, and serve.

VARIATIONS ~ You can use lightly boiled, chilled, then sliced asparagus or raw thinly sliced artichoke hearts instead of the mushrooms, if you prefer.

You can make the same salad using strips of prosciutto cotto instead of the mortadella.

insalata di riso

ITALIAN RICE SALAD

D*ress the vegetables and the rice while they are still warm to absorb the flavors from the other ingredients. This is a summertime classic in Italy, and is very popular on picnics. It is exactly the kind of food you want to eat when the sun is high and temperatures are soaring.*

Serves 4

1¼ cups long-grain Italian rice
2 carrots, cubed
½ cup green beans, diced
1 medium potato, peeled and cubed to the same size
as the carrot cubes
1 small zucchini, cubed
2 tablespoons black or green olives, roughly chopped
4 anchovy fillets, drained, rinsed, drained, dried, and chopped
1 tablespoon capers, rinsed and roughly chopped
1 tablespoon chopped fresh Italian parsley
sea salt and freshly ground black pepper

DRESSING
7 tablespoons extra virgin olive oil
1 tablespoon lemon juice

1 Cook the rice in lightly salted boiling water for 18 minutes, or until tender. Meanwhile, cook the other vegetables in a separate pan until also tender.

2 Drain the rice and all the vegetables thoroughly and place in a large bowl. Add the anchovies, olives, capers, and parsley and using a very large spoon or your hands, mix well until evenly combined.

3 Mix the olive oil and lemon juice together in a separate bowl to make the dressing, then pour over the rice. Mix again and season with salt and pepper to taste.

4 Allow to stand for at least 1 hour before serving. If you need to chill the salad, make sure it is at room temperature when you serve it so that the flavors come through.

insalata di rucola, pere e parmigiano

ARUGULA, PEAR, AND PARMIGIANO SALAD

Arugula, which is actually a herb rather than a salad leaf, has recently become one of the most popular salad vegetables. Here is a classic way to serve arugula with other complementary flavors; the sweet crunch of the pear and the salty taste of the cheese are absolutely perfect with the peppery arugula and a final dash of lemon juice lifts the whole dish.

Serves 4

8 cups fresh arugula leaves
3oz Parmigiano Reggiano
2 small ripe, firm pears
2 to 3 teaspoons lemon juice
2 tablespoons extra virgin olive oil
sea salt and freshly ground black pepper

1 Place the arugula leaves in a large bowl. Shave the cheese with a mandolin or vegetable peeler and add to the bowl.

2 Halve and core the pears. Using a sharp knife, thinly slice the pears (remove the skins only if they are very tough). Place in a separate bowl and cover with lemon juice.

3 Add the pears to the salad. Mix together with your hands, then add the olive oil and salt and pepper to taste. Toss together with salad servers and serve immediately.

VARIATION ~ This salad is also delicious with sorrel used instead of arugula, and walnut oil instead of olive oil.

la caprese

MOZZARELLA AND TOMATO SALAD

This is a classic summer salad from the beautiful island of Capri. Remember not to cut the basil with a knife or with scissors as this will alter the flavor and blacken the leaves. The juice from the tomatoes and the whey from the cheese will tend to seep out and create a lot of liquid around the salad, especially if it is not eaten immediately. In my opinion, this is the best part and must be soaked up with plenty of crusty bread. There is much debate over whether or not one should use buffalo mozzarella. I think the important thing is that the cheese should be really fresh and juicy, whichever milk it is made from. I always make this salad in a salad bowl, but you could also arrange the slices of tomato on a platter and lay the mozzarella on top. Sprinkle the basil over the top of the mozzarella and drizzle the oil over the whole dish. Finish with a sprinkling of salt and pepper.

Serves 4

2 large firm tomatoes
2 mozzarella, drained, each the same size as the tomatoes
6 tablespoons extra virgin olive oil
24 leaves fresh basil, torn into small pieces
sea salt and freshly ground black pepper

1 Using a sharp knife, cut the tomatoes and the mozzarella into even-size slices, cubes or chunks. Place them in a salad bowl and mix them together with your hands. Sprinkle with the olive oil and using a spoon, mix together again.

2 Add the torn basil, season with salt and pepper to taste, and mix again. Allow to stand for about 15 minutes before serving.

SERVING SUGGESTION ~ Do make sure the tomatoes used are not too soft and squashy, nor should they be too green. And don't forget to offer plenty of crusty bread to mop up the juices as you eat.

NOTE ~ When you add salt to the salad, be careful not to add too much, as some mozzarella may already be quite salty.

patate condite

ITALIAN POTATO SALAD

Potato salad is always so much nicer when it isn't chilled. If you must serve it chilled, please remember to dress the potatoes while they are still hot as they will taste much better. Use small, sweet new potatoes for the best results, and make sure they are cooked all the way through—no al dente potatoes please!

Serves 4 to 6

1½lb new potatoes
1 red onion, finely chopped
sea salt and freshly ground black pepper

DRESSING
7 tablespoons extra virgin olive oil
2 tablespoons good-quality white wine vinegar

1 Cook the potatoes in plenty of lightly salted, boiling water until tender, about 15 to 20 minutes. Drain and cut in half while the potatoes are still hot as they will absorb the flavors of the other ingredients.

2 Place the potatoes in a large serving bowl. Add the onion and mix together.

3 Place the olive oil, vinegar, and salt and pepper in a screw-top jar. Close the lid securely and shake together until well blended and emulsified. Taste and adjust the seasoning as required. Alternatively, use a blender.

4 Pour the dressing over the potatoes and onions and toss well to coat. Serve warm or at room temperature.

zucchine condite a scapece

CRISPY ZUCCHINI SALAD

This is a lovely salad, sharp and sweet at the same time. In Naples, where this recipe comes from, the zucchini are laid out in the sun to dry instead of in the oven. I like to serve this salad as part of a cold buffet, alongside cold chicken or thinly sliced cold roast beef. It is all fairly labor intensive and takes a long time to make this properly, but the end result is memorable. Delicious served as a light nibble with drinks.

Serves 4

6 large zucchini
8 tablespoons extra virgin olive oil
a handful of fresh mint leaves
2 garlic cloves
4 tablespoons good-quality red wine vinegar
sea salt

1 Preheat the oven to 300°C. Wash and dry the zucchini, then trim them and cut them lengthwise into even-size slices.

2 Arrange the zucchini slices on lightly greased baking sheets and place in the oven for about 1 hour to dry out completely, but without browning.

3 Heat about 4in of olive oil in a large, wide skillet. Add the dried zucchini and fry quickly until golden. Drain thoroughly on paper towels, then transfer them to a serving dish.

4 Roughly chop the mint and sprinkle over the zucchini. Finely chop the garlic and sprinkle over the zucchini.

5 Sprinkle with the vinegar and salt. Cover and allow to stand for about 1 hour before serving.

NOTE ~ The zucchini is one of Italy's favorite vegetables and is cooked in a variety of ways throughout the nation's regions. In the north, a rich cheese sauce is sometimes used to cover cooked zucchini, whereas the cooks of the southern regions tend to prefer to gently stew their zucchini with onions, garlic, and tomatoes.

During the hot, stifling Italian summer months, there are times when it gets just too hot to eat anything except salad. The Italians have a very scientific approach to their digestive systems and they know when it is wise to eat light, cooling food. So *l'insalata*, salad, has an important place in the hearts of all the Italians I know. This can mean a simple bowl of fresh green leaves, crisp and tender, dressed with just a sprinkling of sea salt and a light drizzle of extra virgin olive oil of the finest quality, or it can mean something much more elaborate and slightly more complex to prepare.

I must confess to being something of a salad aficionado, it is without question my favorite thing to eat when temperatures rise, as I feel it gives such scope to the joy of combining tastes, textures, and colors together. The worst salad I was ever served was a disgusting combination of Persimmons and mayonnaise. It was even worse than that typically boring combination of limp, undressed lettuce, slumped sadly on a plate next to a pile of egg mayonnaise, which in turn is situated too close to sharp, vinegar-laden beet, which is inevitably bleeding copiously into the mayonnaise. To finish off this altogether dull so-called salad, which always looks as bad as it tastes, a watery sliced tomato or two... How very different from fresh Italian salads that look too beautiful to eat, which contain all kinds of seasonal, intensely flavored ingredients, perfectly dressed and all of which work with each other to create a real taste sensation!

One of the main, most basic and important ingredients when creating an Italian salad is extra virgin olive oil. All the southern regions of Italy grow olive trees for olive oil production and, depending upon the region you choose, the oil will be quite different and unique. In the center of the country the regions of Tuscany, Umbria, Lazio, the Marche, and to a much lesser degree Emilia Romagna, all grow olive trees for oil production, and of these Tuscan oil is perhaps the best known. This is oil which is made from olives that are harvested early, hence the oil is rich in chlorophyll, bright green in color, and very grassy and peppery in taste. To the north of the country, the olive trees struggle for survival in the colder weather, however, the olive oil of the Ligurian coastline is to my mind the most sublime oil produced almost anywhere in the world.

Still in the north, the olive trees on the shores of Lake Garda also produce oil that is light and pure, albeit in much smaller quantities than the more prolific production of regions like Puglia or Calabria.

If you have the right oil, all you need to add is a little fresh lemon juice, a pinch of sea salt, and freshly ground black pepper to create a perfectly delicious Italian salad dressing. Lemon juice is a much loved alternative to red or white wine vinegar, especially when the weather is very hot.

Balsamic vinegar has become increasingly popular in the last couple of decades and seems almost set for culinary world domination. This ancient condiment from the solemn city of Modena in Emilia Romagna actually started out as a laxative, sold in pharmacies in the city and surrounding area. I cannot help but smile to myself whenever I see it splashed so liberally over salads and other dishes, practically everywhere I go in the world!

eggs and cheese

fonduta

ITALIAN CHEESE FONDUE

This Italian version of a Swiss cheese fondue can be served either as a dip or on freshly cooked pasta, polenta, or even on top of risotto. It is incredibly rich and filling, so only a very small amount is needed to make you feel really full! My first experience was eating it poured over a huge slab of steaming polenta. It was delicious, and even though I had just walked up a very steep mountainside, I only just about managed to finish my gargantuan portion. Here is the dip version of the recipe.

∽

Serves 4

1lb Fontina cheese, cubed
1 tablespoon all-purpose flour
or 1 tablespoon cornmeal
¾ cup cold milk
4 egg yolks
4 tablespoons butter

1 Mix the cheese and the flour together thoroughly in a deep stainless steel saucepan. Cover with the milk and allow to soften for about 30 minutes.

2 Drain the cheese and place in the top half of a double boiler with the egg yolks and butter. Stir constantly over a low heat until the cheese has melted. The eggs must not be allowed to scramble.

3 As soon as the fonduta is velvety smooth and piping hot, serve it in warmed soup plates or shallow bowls with slices of toasted or fried bread, grissini (breadsticks), or polenta.

frittata al sugo

FRITTATA ~~WITH TOMATO SAUCE~~

This recipe takes me back to very formal and slow lunches at my grandmother's house when I was a little girl. I remember eating this as a first course, sitting in my Nonna's grand dining room with vast napkins, designed for protecting long full skirts, which swamped my whole lower body in starched white damask. Frittata al Sugo was often on the menu, followed usually by some sort of roasted meat.

Serves 4 to 6

FRITTATA
8 large eggs
8oz mozzarella, drained and cubed
1 tablespoon milk
2 tablespoons chopped fresh Italian parsley or basil leaves
3 tablespoons extra virgin olive oil
sea salt and freshly ground black pepper

TOMATO SAUCE
1 medium onion
1 large celery stalk
1 large carrot
4 tablespoons extra virgin olive oil
2 cups fresh or canned tomatoes or passata

TO SERVE
freshly grated Parmigiano Reggiano

1 Beat the eggs together in a large bowl. Add the mozzarella, milk, herbs, and salt and pepper to taste and stir well until thoroughly combined.

2 Heat the olive oil in an 8in skillet until sizzling, then pour in the egg mixture. Pull the mixture into the center, rotating and turning the pan so the egg sets and browns on the underside.

3 After about 5 minutes, or when the mixture feels firm and reasonably set, turn the frittata over by placing a large plate

on top of the skillet and turning the skillet upside down so that the frittata falls onto the plate with the cooked side uppermost.

4 Carefully slide the frittata back into the hot skillet with the cooked side on top and the uncooked side underneath. Shake the skillet to settle the contents and cook for a further 3 or 4 minutes. Slide the frittata out of the pan onto a clean serving plate and allow to cool completely.

5 While the frittata is cooling, make the tomato sauce. Using a sharp knife, chop the onion, celery, and carrot. Pour the oil into the skillet and add the vegetables. Fry very gently and slowly until all the vegetables are soft and the onion becomes transparent. Add the tomatoes and stir thoroughly.

6 Cover and allow to simmer gently for about 30 minutes, stirring frequently.

7 When the frittata is cold, cut it into strips about as wide as your thumb and add it to the tomato sauce. Mix together gently and serve immediately, sprinkled with grated Parmigiano.

In most Italian households the marketing is done twice a day. Everything is freshly cooked for every meal. What the Italian kitchen misses in the form of concentrated meat glazes, fumets of fish and game, the fonds de cuisine *of the French, it makes up for in the extreme freshness and lavishness of its raw materials. It is worth bearing in mind that when an Italian has not the wherewithal to cook one of the traditional extravagant dishes she doesn't attempt to produce an imitation.*

Elizabeth David, *Italian Food*

frittata di verdura

VEGETABLE FRITTATA

The quantity of vegetable to egg varies enormously, depending upon which kind of vegetable you are using. The basic rule of thumb is that there has to be enough egg to hold the whole dish together, but there must be enough vegetable content for the vegetable to form the main part of the finished dish. I tend to use about two thirds vegetable and one third eggs. Be very careful not to add too much cheese, as this will cause the frittata to stick and make it impossible to turn over successfully. The amount of time it takes to cook the frittata will depend on how thick it is and what kind of pan you are using.

Serves 4 to 6

6–10oz vegetable of your choice, such as Swiss chard, spinach, zucchini, or onions (boiled, steamed, or sautéed, then carefully drained of any liquid)
6 eggs, beaten
⅔ cup freshly grated Parmigiano Reggiano
4 tablespoons olive oil
sea salt and freshly ground black pepper

1 Whatever vegetable you choose to put into the frittata, it must be as dry as possible. This makes the frittata easy to slice into wedges once cooked.

2 If using green leaf vegetables such as Swiss chard or spinach, squeeze the water out of the cooked leaves before finely chopping. Other vegetables need to be thoroughly drained of any liquid.

3 Mix the hot or cold vegetable into the beaten eggs, then add the Parmigiano and salt and pepper to taste. Mix well.

4 Heat the olive oil in a wide, shallow skillet until very hot, then pour in the egg mixture.

5 Shake the skillet to flatten and even out the frittata, pulling the liquid egg into the center as you work. Cook until the underside is browned and firm.

6 Turn the frittata over by placing a large plate or lid on top of the skillet and turning the skillet upside down so that the frittata falls onto the plate with the cooked side uppermost.

7 Carefully slide the frittata back into the hot skillet with the cooked side on top and the uncooked side underneath. Cook until golden brown and firm on the underside. Slide out onto a clean, flat platter and serve hot or cold.

NOTE It goes without saying that the prerequisite for any successful dish with eggs is the freshness of the egg itself. To check if an egg is as fresh as the packaging or the vendor claims it to be, try this simple old-fashioned test. Place an egg into a bowl containing enough slightly salted cold water to submerge it. If the egg stays horizontal, it is fresh. If it turns itself vertical, the egg has lost its freshness.

Using eggs or cheese either together or separately, is always a good alternative to cooking meat or fish for a satisfying main course. We generally eat less meat these days, so the popularity of dishes containing little or no meat increases. At the same time, those containing a combination of vegetables with either cheese and/or eggs become more widespread. Take for example the perfectly simple flat omelet, called frittata, which can be made with cooked vegetables, often perked up with a little cheese.

I think all of us are guilty of saving up tiny pieces of cheese in our refrigerator, bits that are too mean to be part of the cheese board, and yet too valuable to just throw away. In the case of any of these dishes, leftover bits of cheese can enhance and improve the flavor of many simple combinations.

Italy has a wonderful range of cheeses, of which Parmigiano Reggiano and Grana Padano are perhaps the best known. Both of them are hard grating cheeses with a gritty texture, which becomes more pronounced the older the cheese becomes. Mascarpone and ricotta are cheeses which, like butter, are made out of the by-products of these hard cheeses, using the cream which is skimmed off the top in the case of the former, and the reboiled curds in the case of the latter.

mozzarella in carrozza

DEEP-FRIED MOZZARELLA SANDWICHES

When we were kids growing up in Italy we would enjoy this dish as a snack. Our appetites never seemed to lessen in those days and our afternoon snack, despite huge lunches and enormous dinners, was vital to survival! It is quite a heavy dish, given that it is deep-fried bread and cheese, so it needs to be served either on its own or with very light components to make up a meal. The name means that the mozzarella is in a golden carriage, like Cinderella!

Serves 4

8 slices white bread, crusts removed
1½ teaspoons anchovy paste
8 thick slices mozzarella
3 eggs
sunflower oil to deep-fry
freshly ground black pepper

TO SERVE
tomato sauce (optional)

1 Lay 4 slices of the bread out on a board and spread each one with anchovy paste.

2 Cover the anchovy paste with slices of mozzarella. Season with a little pepper and place the other slices of bread on top. Firmly push down on each sandwich with your hand to press it together.

3 Beat the eggs in a large bowl. Place the sandwiches into the beaten egg and leave to soak for about 15 minutes (you may need to use more than one bowl to leave the sandwiches soaking at the same time).

4 Meanwhile, pour about 3in depth of sunflower oil into a wide, deep skillet and heat until a small cube of bread, dropped onto the surface of the oil sizzles instantly.

5 Add the sandwiches to the hot oil and deep-fry until crisp and golden on both sides. Remove the sandwiches with a spatula and drain well on paper towels. Serve piping hot with a bowl of tomato sauce if desired.

uova al forno

BAKED EGGS

A really easy and satisfying way to serve eggs. This makes a perfect addition to a brunch menu or an easy supper dish. As always when making something as deliciously simple as this, it is very important that your basic ingredients should be the very best available. The olive oil, for example, must be extra virgin and rich in flavor. The tomatoes, though canned, cannot be sour and watery, and the eggs should be free range and as fresh as possible.

serves 4

1 medium red onion, chopped fine
3 tablespoons extra virgin olive oil
2 cups canned chopped tomatoes
a handful of fresh basil leaves
8 eggs
sea salt and freshly ground black pepper

TO SERVE
salad
crusty bread

1 Preheat the oven to 350°F. Place the onion in a saucepan with 2 tablespoons of the olive oil. Fry until the onion is soft. Add the tomatoes and stir together. Add half the basil leaves. Season with salt and pepper to taste.

2 Cover and simmer very slowly for about 30 minutes, stirring occasionally. Remove the pan from the heat.

3 Lightly grease an ovenproof dish, then pour in the sauce with the remaining oil.

4 Break the eggs into the dish on top of the sauce, making hollows in the sauce for the eggs to sit in. Season with salt and pepper and sprinkle with the torn basil leaves.

5 Bake in the oven for about 10 minutes or until the eggs are just set but the yolks are still runny. Serve immediately with salad and crusty bread.

vegetables

carciofi alla romana

BRAISED ARTICHOKES WITH GARLIC, LEMON, AND MINT

Artichokes are my favorite vegetable, so any recipe for them always manages to thrill me, but this is the recipe I remember from my years growing up and going to school in Rome. I lived in the area around the Borghese gardens, overlooking the green treetops of the park with the cupola of St. Peter perfectly silhouetted against the most glorious sunsets imaginable. I learned to strip and clean artichokes here, sitting around a central bucket filled with cold water and cut lemons, amazed then as I am now at how much of the vegetable seems to be wasted in the long process of stripping and trimming. But the guilty feeling of all that waste evaporates the moment you start to eat them, especially when tenderly prepared as here. If you have never prepared an artichoke for braising, let me reassure you that the huge pile of detritus at the end of the process is how it should be!

Serves 6

2 lemons, halved
12 artichokes
12 garlic cloves, sliced thin
a large handful of fresh mint
1 small lemon, cut into small segments
1 cup water
¼ cup olive oil
sea salt and freshly ground black pepper

1 Fill a bowl large enough to hold the prepared artichokes with cold water and squeeze the juice of half a lemon into it. Place the halved lemons into the water.

2 Prepare the artichokes by trimming the stalk and peeling away the tough outer leaves. Cut off the tops and remove the choke by scooping it out with a teaspoon. Place the hearts into the bowl of cold water.

3 When all the artichokes are ready to cook, remove them from the water and dry them with a dish towel, then rub them all over with the quartered lemons and place them in a wide saucepan or baking pan.

4 Place a few slices of garlic inside each artichoke and strip the leaves off the mint. Distribute the mint and the lemon inside and among the artichokes.

5 Season generously with salt and pepper. Pour over the water and oil. Cover and leave to simmer gently for about 30 minutes, or until almost soft all the way through.

6 Turn the artichokes over to help them to finish cooking and baste occasionally. Don't let them dry out, keep adding water or white wine as necessary. Serve hot or cold.

VARIATION ~ Artichokes come in all shapes and sizes, and there are countless variations on the basic braising recipe, which mainly consist of changing the ingredients used to fill the interior of the artichoke. This is one of my favorite dishes, and one I often serve as an appetizer, either hot or cold.

Everyone eats well in Italy. Eating well is a sign of well being, of the normal functioning of a family.

Giorgio Locatelli, *Tony and Giorgio*

cardi al forno

BAKED CARDOONS

The strange looking cardoon has a wonderful taste, which belies its bizarre appearance. It can be very stringy, so needs careful preparation before cooking. It is one of those vegetables which improves in flavor after the frost has got to it and, like its cousin the artichoke, it tends to discolor very quickly.

❧

Serves 4

2 lemons, quartered
1¼lb cardoons
4 tablespoons olive oil
1⅓ cups freshly grated Parmigiano Reggiano
sea salt and freshly ground black pepper

1 Fill a large bowl with cold water and squeeze the juice of a lemon quarter into it. Place the quartered lemons into the water. Preheat the oven to 400°F.

2 Remove all the leaves from the cardoons and strip away all the fibrous strings that run through the length of each stick with a sharp knife.

3 Cut the sticks into 2in sections and drop them into the bowl of cold water.

4 When all the cardoons are prepared, bring a large pan of salted water to a boil. Drain the cardoons and drop them into the pan of boiling water. Cover and simmer for 30 minutes until just tender, then drain again.

5 Grease an ovenproof dish large enough to hold all the cardoons in a single, overlapping layer.

6 Sprinkle the cardoons with the remaining olive oil, cover generously with the Parmigiano Reggiano and place in the oven to heat through and melt the cheese. Serve hot.

carote in padella

BRAISED CARROTS

Whenever we had carrots at home in Italy, they were either cooked like this or served grated in a salad. The fact that the carrots had been pulled from our own vegetable garden made a big difference, but I still think this is a nicer way of preparing a cooked carrot than simply boiling it. Boiled carrots, at home in Italy, had a vague connection with upset stomachs! Whenever anyone complained of having a "funny tummy" (the Italian word was much more entertaining and descriptive, but slightly vulgar!) the household remedy was always plates of boiled carrots with boiled rice.

Serves 6

2½ cups carrots, sliced thickly into rounds
1 to 2 tablespoons unsalted butter
1 heaping tablespoon chopped fresh parsley
sea salt and freshly ground black pepper

1 Bring a saucepan of salted water to a boil. Add the carrots and boil quickly for 5 minutes. Drain the carrots thoroughly.

2 Melt the butter in a large skillet. Add the drained carrots and season with salt and pepper to taste.

3 Cook for an additional 15 minutes, or until tender, stirring occasionally and adding extra water as necessary. The carrots should be tender and slightly browned. Sprinkle with the chopped parsley and serve hot.

cavolo all'aglio

BRAISED CABBAGE WITH GARLIC

In my childhood home in Tuscany, we would always have cabbage when pork was served, and it seemed to me that the two always went together! It has to be said that this very easy, classical way of cooking cabbage is indeed delicious with juicy pork chops or succulent roasted pork, though it does work very well with other meats too. Incidentally, in Tuscany we never ate pork in the summer time, it was always a meat reserved for the cold days of winter, because it was considered too hard to digest in the heat, I think....

Serves 6

4 tablespoons olive oil
4 garlic cloves, roughly chopped
1 Savoy cabbage, roughly shredded
sea salt and freshly ground black pepper

1 Heat the olive oil in a large, shallow saucepan. Add the garlic and fry until the garlic is just turning golden brown. Add the cabbage and stir together very thoroughly.

2 Cover the pan with a lid and leave to wilt completely, stirring occasionally.

3 As soon as the cabbage has wilted and has begun to color slightly around the edges season generously with salt and pepper. Serve hot.

VARIATION ~ Exactly the same cooking method can be used to cook silver beet/Swiss chard, kale or other kinds of cabbage—except red cabbage, which takes much longer to cook and is far better suited to being combined with sugar, spices, and vinegar than garlic and olive oil.

fagioli in umido

STEWED BEANS

This dish works well with either fresh cannellini or cranberry beans. However, if fresh beans are not available, dried ones can be used instead. I like to serve these beans alongside some broiled sausages, with a roast pork or beef dish, or even with game. These stewed beans are also absolutely delicious with braised squid. This recipe can also be used to top crostini or bruschetta as an original version of beans on toast!

Serves 4

2¼lb fresh cranberry or cannellini beans in their pods
3 or 4 tablespoons olive oil
3 garlic cloves, crushed
a pinch of ground black pepper
sea salt

1 Drain and rinse the beans, place them in a large saucepan and cover them in cold water. Bring to a boil and boil fast for 5 minutes.

2 Drain and rinse, then return to the pan and cover with fresh water. Simmer gently for about 7 minutes until tender.

3 Heat the olive oil in a skillet. Add the garlic and fry gently. When the garlic is golden brown, add the pepper and beans. Stir well.

4 Add just enough water to cover if required, then simmer gently for an additional 20 minutes. Taste and adjust the seasoning if necessary, just before serving.

NOTE ~ If using dried beans, soak in cold water overnight, drain and rinse, then boil fast in fresh water for 5 minutes, drain and rinse again, and use as fresh.

cipolline all'agro dolce

BRAISED SWEET AND SOUR ONIONS

This is one of my favorite vegetable dishes and is traditionally made using those marvelous flat little ready-peeled button onions which you can so conveniently buy in Italy. If you can't find these onions (called borettane) you can use pearl onions or small shallots instead. You can use less or more vinegar for this recipe, partly because of personal taste, but also because I find the acidity level in good-quality vinegar sometimes varies wildly.

Serves 4

2 tablespoons sunflower oil
1lb small onions, peeled
3 tablespoons balsamic vinegar
2 tablespoons white wine vinegar
2 tablespoons granulated sugar
sea salt and freshly ground black pepper

1 Heat the sunflower oil in a wide, deep skillet for about 3 minutes, then add the onions. Toss them in the hot oil until they begin to brown, then add both vinegars, sugar, and seasoning.

2 Stir and simmer, uncovered, until the acidic fumes from the vinegars have burned off. Add just enough water to barely cover and reduce the heat.

3 Cover the skillet with a lid and simmer gently for about 30 to 40 minutes, stirring frequently.

4 If there is too much liquid left at the end, when the onions are tender and soft without being mushy, remove the lid then remove the onions with a slotted spoon and place in a serving dish. Increase the heat to reduce the excess liquid. This can be poured back over the cooked onions. Serve hot or cold.

fagiolini al pomodoro

STEWED GREEN BEANS

There is a tradition in Italy of cooking vegetables such as green beans until they are softened and stewed with other ingredients, often with tomato. This goes against the grain with those people who prefer their green beans crisp. However, this is a good way of cooking green beans that do not have much taste to begin with!

Serves 4

4 cups green beans, topped and tailed
5 tablespoons olive oil
1 large red onion, sliced thin
1 heaping tablespoon tomato paste diluted in about
4 tablespoons hot water
1 teaspoon fennel seeds, lightly crushed
sea salt and freshly ground black pepper

1 Bring a large saucepan of lightly salted water to a boil. Add the beans and cook until just about tender.

2 Meanwhile, heat the olive oil in a large skillet. Add the onion and fry until soft. Then stir in the tomato paste and crushed fennel seeds.

3 Drain the beans thoroughly and add them to the skillet. Mix everything together and season with salt and pepper to taste.

4 Cover and cook through for an additional 20 minutes, then serve. This is also delicious cold, bearing in mind that the flavor of the fennel seeds will increase as the beans absorb more of the sauce.

VARIATION ~ If the taste of fennel is not to your liking, simply leave it out. This is a very good way of using up late season beans, which tend to be a little tough. The long cooking process makes even very tired beans tasty.

la parmigiana

LAYERED VEGETABLE AND MOZZARELLA CASSEROLE WITH PARMIGIANO

This wonderful, rich and luscious vegetable dish is layered like a lasagna, and always tastes so much better the day after you've made it! Although the name of this dish might suggest that the dish comes from the fair city of Parma, this is confusing because the origins of the dish actually lie in and around Naples. I was first taught how to make the dish in the very traditional Neapolitan way—which calls specifically for long, oblong eggplants—in the town of Poistano at the home of one of the region's most highly respected gastronomes.

This recipe is the traditional and classic version using eggplants, but you can also make it with zucchini, potatoes, artichoke bases, or a combination of any of those. You can griddle or bake the eggplant slices instead of frying them if you are worried about the finished dish becoming too greasy. Because eggplants can contain bitter juices, which might spoil the overall flavor of the dish, I recommend that you salt the sliced eggplants before cooking, as explained in step 3 of this recipe.

Serves 4

3 long eggplants, washed and cut lengthwise into
rounds, ends discarded
1 cup sunflower oil
12oz mozzarella, drained and sliced
2⅔ cups freshly grated Parmigiano Reggiano
2 handfuls of fresh basil leaves
sea salt and freshly ground black pepper

TOMATO SAUCE
3 to 5 tablespoons richly flavoured extra virgin olive oil
2 garlic cloves, thinly sliced or crushed
1lb fresh tomatoes, peeled and deseeded
or 2 cups canned or puréed tomatoes

1 Make the tomato sauce first. Heat the olive oil in a heavy saucepan or skillet. Add the garlic and fry very gently until soft. Pour in the tomatoes and stir carefully. Cover and allow to simmer for about 20 minutes, or until the sauce is glossy and thick. Season with salt and pepper to taste and cover. Remove the pan from the heat, and keep warm.

2 An alternative method is to heat the oil in a saucepan or skillet. Add the garlic and fry until browned, then remove and discard. Pour the tomatoes into the garlic flavored oil. Finish the sauce with a handful of fresh basil, cover and allow to cool before use.

3 Sprinkle the eggplant slices with salt and lay them in a large colander. Cover with a plate and put a weight on top of the plate. Stand the colander in the sink for 1 hour to let the bitter juices of the eggplants drain away.

4 Preheat the oven to 350°F. Rinse the eggplants under cold running water and pat dry with paper towels. Heat the sunflower oil in a wide skillet. Add the eggplant slices and quickly fry until soft and golden brown.

5 Drain them carefully and thoroughly on paper towels to remove as much of the oil as possible.

6 Use some olive oil to grease a shallow ovenproof dish. Place a little of the tomato sauce on the base of the dish, then cover with a layer of slightly overlapping eggplant slices.

7 Cover with a layer of mozzarella, a layer of tomato sauce, a generous sprinkling of Parmigiano Reggiano, and a few torn basil leaves. Repeat until the dish is filled and all the ingredients have been used.

8 Bake in the oven for about 40 minutes, then remove from the oven and allow to stand for about 5 minutes before serving.

The taste of basil, parmesan and olive oil, the smell of garlic frying with sage and rosemary, bring back the brilliant light and pure primary colours, with images of Italy and feelings of joy and enchantment.

Claudia Roden, *The Food of Italy*

finocchi brasati

BRAISED FENNEL

Fennel is used a great deal in Italian cooking, either raw or cooked, in soups, risotto, and salads or as an accompanying vegetable. Here is the simplest and most classic way of serving it cooked as a side vegetable. Fennel is one of the easiest vegetables to select by gender. The female, which is much sleeker and sinuous than the stocky, stubby male, has a much stronger liquorice taste. In Italy, fennel is always selected according to its gender and while the female is considered suitable for salads, only the male is ever used for cooking.

Serves 6

6 fennel bulbs, trimmed
2½ tablespoons unsalted butter
sea salt and freshly ground black pepper

TO SERVE
2 tablespoons freshly grated Parmigiano Reggiano

1 Using a sharp knife, quarter the fennel bulbs. Bring a saucepan of salted water to a boil. Add the fennel and boil for about 6 minutes, or until just tender. Drain thoroughly.

2 Melt the butter in a wide skillet. Add the fennel quarters, season with salt and pepper, and baste with the butter, adding enough water to prevent them from burning.

3 Cover and continue to cook through, turning them frequently so that they brown slightly on all sides. Serve hot, sprinkled with freshly grated Parmigiano Reggiano.

SERVING SUGGESTION ~ Alternatively, cover the fennel completely in grated cheese then place under a preheated broiler until browned. Serve immediately.

patatine arrosto

ITALIAN ROAST POTATOES

No subject seems to get people quite as excited and opinionated around the Sunday roast as the subject of how to cook the best roast potatoes! Goose fat, duck fat, variety of potato, rolling in flour, parboiling... on and on it goes! This very Italian version is crisp, crunchy, moist on the inside, and deliciously scented by the lemon and rosemary.

Serves 6

**6 large or 12 small potatoes, peeled and cut into
cherry-sized cubes
8 garlic cloves, unpeeled
1 lemon, cut into 8 pieces
juice of ½ lemon
1 to 2 large fresh rosemary sprigs, broken into pieces
8 tablespoons extra virgin olive oil
sea salt and freshly ground black pepper**

1 Drop the cubed potatoes into a bowl of cold water and allow to stand for at least 2 hours. Drain, rinse and dry on a dish towel.

2 Preheat the oven to 400°F. Place the dry potato cubes in a metal roasting pan and add the garlic cloves, lemon pieces, lemon juice, rosemary, and salt and pepper to taste.

3 Using your hands, mix everything together, then add the olive oil and mix again.

4 Season again with salt, then roast in the oven for about 40 to 45 minutes, shaking the pan and turning the potatoes twice as they cook. They should be crisp and golden brown. Serve piping hot.

VARIATION ~ You can add a handful or two of cherry tomatoes to cook through for the second half of the cooking time, and serve with eggs and a crisp green salad for a very quick supper.

puree di patate

ITALIAN MASHED POTATOES

Making Italian mashed potato is a real labor of love, it takes a great deal of effort to produce a purée that is so fluffy and smooth.

Serves 6

2¼lb potatoes, unpeeled
4 tablespoons unsalted butter
milk
sea salt

1 Bring a large saucepan of salted water to a boil. Add the potatoes and boil until tender, about 20 minutes. Drain, peel, and push twice through a food mill on medium hole setting.

2 Place the purée in the saucepan and dry out slightly over a low heat, stirring the butter through the purée.

3 Add enough milk to make the purée light and airy and work it hard with a wooden spoon to make it as fluffy as possible. Be careful not to over work it or you'll break down the starch and the purée will become very sticky and gloopy. Serve hot.

pomodori arraganati

BAKED TOMATOES

S low roasted, herb-coated tomatoes are served as part of an antipasti or side vegetable. Delicious with roast chicken.

Serves 6

6 ripe and juicy fist-sized round or plum tomatoes
about 10 tablespoons olive oil
9 teaspoons fresh breadcrumbs
3 garlic cloves, chopped fine
¼ teaspoon salt
1 teaspoon dried oregano
3 tablespoons chopped fresh parsley
freshly ground black pepper

1 Preheat the oven to 325°F. Wash and dry the tomatoes thoroughly. Cut them in half and remove the stalks. Grease an ovenproof dish and arrange the tomatoes side by side.

2 Mix the bread crumbs, garlic, seasoning, oregano, and parsley together. Bind lightly together, then use to coat the cut half of each tomato thoroughly.

3 Drizzle with a little more olive oil and bake in the oven for about 40 minutes, or until the tomatoes are soft and tender. Serve hot or cold.

ALL ABOUT VEGETABLES

When it comes to the subject of vegetables, as far as all Italian cooks are concerned there is simply no limit to the number of amazing flavor and texture combinations. Italy's climate and soil conditions mean that literally hundreds of different varieties of vegetables grow all over the country. Out of these precious riches, countless recipes are created either using vegetables as the central ingredient or as one of many other ingredients. Vegetables are often served as a very simple accompaniment to a main course. They tend to be cooked in the most uncomplicated way, either boiled or fried, with no more than a squeeze of lemon and a drizzle of olive oil to finish them off.

The collection of recipes in this chapter contains both "complete meal" vegetable dishes, and some that are designed to accompany the main course. In all cases I have tried to make the recipes very simple and easy to cook and shop for, but nevertheless interesting and above all classically Italian.

Of all the vegetables used in Italian dishes, tomatoes must be the most loved and used. Fresh tomatoes are used all the way through their summer season. At the end of the season, when the tomatoes are at their sweetest and their canes can barely support their weight, the bottling begins. This is a ritual that takes place at the end of the summer and gathers families together to make enough tomato sauce and bottled tomatoes to see everybody through the long winter.

Originally, tomatoes found their way into the hearts and onto the tables of Italians from Naples. When the tomato was brought back to Italy from the New World, it was considered to be the evil apple from the Garden of Eden and as such was declared dangerous and toxic. It took almost 200 years before the tomato found its way into the kitchen, where it was first used to make a sauce for pasta. Tomatoes as a topping for pizza took a little longer to evolve.

Going to an Italian market, at any time of the year is an education in itself as far as gaining an understanding of just how wide the range of available vegetables really is. Yet all of them are only available when in season, so that the sense of anticipation is never lost. Early season vegetables are called *primizie* and appear at the very beginning of their season and are sold at premium prices by vendors who specialize in them.

Growing up in Tuscany, I became addicted at a very early age to the joy of eating vegetables that are as fresh as possible, kissed by the sun, and picked only minutes before eating them. The only way to achieve this kind of intensity of flavor is to grow your own, something I would always urge you to do, even if it is only a window box or a few flowerpots with some tomato plants in them. There is nothing like the taste of vegetables that have been grown with love and care.

pasta

la sfoglia

FRESH PASTA

La sfoglia *is the generic Italian term for a finely rolled,
almost transparent fine sheet of pasta or pastry. The verb
sfogliane means to leaf through (as in a book) and thus brings
to mind the idea of light paper pages rustling softly. In Italy, it
is now rare to find anybody making fresh pasta on a daily
basis; it is a practice saved for festival days and holidays, when
there are enough pairs of hands in the kitchen to help with the
work. The quantities are given per person, because that is how
quantities of pasta are calculated—in "eggs worth"—one egg
being enough for one person.*

Serves 1

**1 cup all-purpose plain flour
1 large egg
salt**

1 Place the flour in a pile on the countertop and plunge your fist into the center to make a hollow. Break the egg into the hole and add a pinch of salt.

2 Using your fingers or a fork, beat the egg thoroughly, then begin to knead it roughly into the flour. Using your hands, knead everything together. This is not like making pastry, so this is not the moment for a delicate approach, but if you are too heavy handed you will cause the dough to dry out too much and it will never roll out smoothly!

3 Continue to knead until you have a really smooth, pliable ball of dough. Rest under a clean cloth for about 20 minutes. This will relax the gluten and make the dough more manageable.

4 Roll out the dough on a lightly floured countertop as thinly as possible with a strong long rolling pin. Continue to roll it over and over again until the dough is elastic, smooth, and shiny. It should cool down considerably as you work it, and you will feel it dropping in temperature as you go along.

5 When it is ready the sheet of dough will feel like a brand new, wrung out, damp chamois leather, but must not be brittle. When you are not working with the dough cover with a slightly damp clean cloth to keep it moist.

6 Alternatively, use a pasta machine. Knead the egg and flour into a rough textured ball of dough. Rest the dough

for 20 minutes, then cover it with a very slightly damp cloth. Break off a piece of dough about the size of a small fist and flatten it out with your hands.

7 Push the dough through the widest setting on your pasta machine and fold this in half and then repeat. Do this three times. Move the machine down to the next setting. Repeat another three times. Continue in this way, changing the setting after every three times until you hear the pasta snap as it is going between the rollers. At this point you can forget about folding it in half each time as the surface tension is now correct.

8 Continue to wind it through the rollers to the last or penultimate setting on the machine, depending on how fine you want it to be. Lay the sheet of pasta carefully on a floured countertop.

9 Take another lump of dough the size of a small fist and begin again. Repeat with all the pasta. Keep an eye on the sheets of pasta you have rolled out. Place them on a floured countertop to dry, but remember they will not be easy to cut if they are too dry. Cover with slightly damp, clean cloths to keep them moist.

10 You can cut your pasta into the desired shape as soon as it is dry enough to roll up without it sticking to itself. Once cut, you can use the pasta immediately or let it dry out further. If you are making a filled pasta shape such as ravioli you must use soft, moist pasta otherwise it will not be possible to close each one securely. In this case, fill the pasta immediately, then leave the shapes to dry.

TO FREEZE FRESH PASTA ~ Open freeze on trays, then place in bags and label. Keeps for about 1 month once frozen.

NOTE ~ Bear in mind that no two batches of flour are identical, and that no two eggs are ever quite the same either so if you do end up having to add more egg or more flour to your mixture, it is not an indication of failure on your part! I do think that trying to explain how to make fresh pasta is very hard to do and must be almost impossible to really grasp for the reader. It is better to go to a pasta-making class with an expert if you can, so that you can see for yourself what actually happens during this magical process!

This quintessential Italian ingredient has become one of the most popular foodstuffs the world has ever known. There are quite literally hundreds of different pasta shapes, and many thousands of dressings and sauces to go with them. Once you have mastered the idea of boiling and draining pasta, pouring a sauce over it and tossing them together, there is no limit to what you can decide to put onto pasta if you wish. There is a definite relationship between the shape of pasta you choose to cook and the sauce or dressing that goes with it. The idea is that when you finish eating, there should be only a little bit of the sauce left on the plate because the shape of pasta chosen needs to have the ability to embrace and gather up as much of whatever is dressing it as you eat, rather than falling off. So as a general (very general) rule, choose smooth sauces with long pasta shapes and lumpy sauces with short and stubby shapes. But having said that, there are exceptions to the rule and many people just prefer one shape and refuse to eat any other, no matter what the sauce is.

There are two basic types of pasta, which are widely available everywhere. The first is dried durum wheat pasta, consisting of durum wheat flour and water, mixed, cut and dried in factory conditions. This is the pasta you cannot make at home and includes spaghetti, bucatini, penne, fusilli and about six hundred other shapes.

Fresh pasta is made with ordinary flour and eggs, kneaded together to make a softer, richer, more luxurious pasta. This can be made at home and includes: tagliatelle, fettuccine, cannelloni, lasagna and many others. In Italy fresh pasta is the one usually saved for specific occasions, simply because it is more special than the ordinary every day variety.

Dried durum wheat pasta in itself is very good for you and not as fattening as one might think. A plate of durum wheat spaghetti dressed with a very basic and simple tomato, olive oil, garlic, and basil sauce contains just under 300 calories. With a fat-free sauce like the one on page 124, the calories are even fewer.

Of course, a plate of pasta covered in a creamy, butter filled, alcohol laden sauce is packed with calories and all sorts of other extras that are not so good if you are trying to lose weight. In fact, some pasta dishes are so clogged with cream and butter and cheese that they actually contain more calories and fat than a huge slab of chocolate cake.

il ragu alla bolognese

SLOW-COOKED BOLOGNESE SAUCE

This slow-cooked sauce is a very long way from the ground beef and canned tomato version that we have somehow grown to know by the same name! Note the quantity of tomato paste used in comparison to the huge quantity of meat. Incidentally, to achieve the right texture, it is essential to chop the meat by hand and not in a food processor.

Serves 4

4oz pork loin, boned
4oz beef steak, boned
4oz prosciutto crudo
4 tablespoons unsalted butter
1 carrot, chopped fine
1 celery stalk, finely chopped
1 onion, chopped fine
2oz pancetta or bacon, chopped fine
1 heaping tablespoon tomato paste diluted with 1 glass hot water
1½ ladles hot broth or water
4oz chicken livers, washed, trimmed, and chopped fine
6 tablespoons heavy or light cream
1 small truffle, cleaned and sliced thin, optional
sea salt and freshly ground black pepper
14oz tagliatelle or other fresh pasta of your choice

1 Using a heavy cook's knife, finely chop the pork loin, beef steak, and prosciutto crudo.

2 Melt half the butter in a large skillet. Add the carrot, celery, onion, and pancetta or bacon and fry for 5 to 6 minutes, stirring. Add the chopped meats and stir together to seal all over.

3 Add the diluted tomato paste. Season with salt and pepper to taste. Stir thoroughly, cover, and allow to simmer as slowly as possible for about 3 hours. Make sure it does not dry out.

4 Stir frequently and keep adding a little hot broth or water. After about 3 hours, when all the meat is tender, add the chopped chicken livers and simmer for an additional 5 minutes.

5 Stir in the cream and the truffle, if using. Allow to stand until required or use immediately. It is best made a day or so ahead and reheated gently at the last moment. Serve with freshly cooked tagliatelle.

NOTE ~ Don't be tempted to add truffle oil instead of a truffle, because it is very unlikely that the truffle oil contains even the merest trace of real truffle. The only possible substitute is a knob of truffle butter instead.

il sugo di pomodoro

TOMATO SAUCE

I am going to give you three completely different tomato sauces for pasta, as I believe it to be essential for so many aspects of Italian cooking. This first sauce can also be bottled in sterilized bottles for the winter. It contains no fat and is reliant on the flavor of the tomatoes and the other ingredients. The second sauce begins with a classical soffritto, a mixture of onion, carrot, and celery, which is gently fried until soft. Tomatoes are then added. The third is the quickest and with the least ingredients, and has a garlic base. Of course there are many other variations, but the most important thing to remember is that the tomatoes you choose for your sauce must be of the best possible quality as this will give you the best results—a watery tomato, fresh or canned, will give you a sauce with less flavor.

Serves 6 (once reduced, makes about 2 cups)

**2¼lb fresh plum tomatoes, peeled and quartered or 4½ cups
canned plum tomatoes, drained and quartered
1 small onion, quartered
1 carrot, quartered
1 celery stalk, quartered
1 large fresh parsley sprig
7 fresh basil leaves
3 tablespoons olive oil
sea salt**

1 Place all the ingredients except the salt in a saucepan.
Cover and bring to a boil, then allow to simmer for
30 minutes. Remove the lid and simmer for an additional 20
minutes, until most of the liquid has evaporated.

2 Remove the pan from the heat and push through a food mill
or strainer. Alternatively, process in a food processor until
smooth and then strain into a bowl.

3 Return the sauce to a boil and reduce until thickened. Season
with salt and pepper to taste once you have achieved the
texture you like. Either use immediately or allow to cool and
refrigerate until required.

**NOTE ~ If you want to enrich the flavor and texture add either
1 tablespoon of unsalted butter or 2 tablespoons of extra virgin
olive oil to the sauce as soon as it has been heated through. The
idea is not to cook the butter or oil, but just to stir it through, so
do this off the heat.**

l'arrabbiata

TOMATO AND CHILI SAUCE

Recipes using dried red chile are more popular and appear more frequently the further south of home you travel. Basilicata, the region in the instep of the "boot," definitely has the hottest recipes in chili terms anywhere in the country. The literal translation of this recipe is "angry," meaning fiery, and you can add as much chile as you want, so increasing the rage level you can call your sauce furiosa (furious) or allo strillo (at screaming pitch), and so on!

Serves 4

4 tablespoons extra virgin olive oil
4 garlic cloves, chopped fine
1 to 4 dried red chiles (depending upon how hot
you want the sauce)
2¼ cups canned chopped tomatoes, drained if necessary
14oz penne
1 teaspoon chopped fresh parsley
sea salt

1 Heat the olive oil in a large saucepan. Add the garlic and chile and fry briefly until the garlic and chile are blackened. Remove and discard them and add the tomatoes to the pan. Season with salt and simmer for about 20 minutes.

2 Bring a large saucepan of salted water to a boil. Add the penne, stir, then cover. Return to a boil, and cook until al dente. Remove or adjust the lid once the water is boiling again.

3 Drain the pasta and return to the pan. Pour over the sauce and mix together.

4 Transfer to a warmed serving dish and sprinkle with the parsley before serving. Cheese is not normally served with this recipe, however if you or your guests insist on having cheese choose aged, peppery pecorino.

la puttanesca

ROMAN WHORE'S SAUCE

The overall rough texture and intense flavors of this very rustic sauce are what gives it the famous name. Although delicious and traditional with pasta, this classic sauce is also wonderful served with broiled fish. I have suggested only one clove of garlic, although you can add up to three or more if you prefer. You can also increase the quantities of any of the other ingredients for an intense combination of tastes.

Serves 4

8 tablespoons extra virgin olive oil
1 garlic clove
3 anchovy fillets (either salted or canned in oil,
rinsed and dried)
1 small dried red chile, chopped fine
1 tablespoon rinsed and dried chopped salted capers
1 cup canned chopped tomatoes
a large pinch of dried oregano
¼ cup dry white wine
a handful of stoned black olives
sea salt and freshly ground black pepper

TO SERVE
freshly cooked pasta, such as spaghetti

1 Heat half the olive oil in a large skillet. Add the garlic, anchovy fillets, and the dried chile, and cook until the anchovy dissolves.

2 Add the capers and tomatoes and stir together thoroughly. Simmer for a few minutes, then add the oregano, salt and pepper to taste, wine, and olives.

3 Stir and let simmer gently for at least 15 minutes. It can be left for a little longer if needed.

4 Serve over freshly cooked pasta, traditionally spaghetti, tossed together with a little extra olive oil.

pasta alla carbonara

BACON AND EGG SAUCE WITH PASTA

This has to be one of the most bastardized of all the pasta sauce recipes. The classic version is this one: no cream, no mushrooms! It is very important that the pancetta should be very fatty and that the liquid, hot fat should very much be a part of the dish, so don't be tempted to pour it away when frying. Traditionally, this dish is always made with pecorino, but you can use Parmigiano Reggiano if you prefer.

Serves 4

14oz dried bucatini or spaghetti
6oz cubed pancetta
3 eggs
5 tablespoons freshly grated pecorino or Parmigiano Reggiano
salt and freshly ground black pepper

1 Bring a large saucepan of salted water to a boil. Add the pasta, stir, cover, and return to a boil. Remove or adjust the lid once the water is boiling again.

2 While the pasta is cooking, fry the pancetta in a very hot skillet until crisp and running freely with the fat.

3 Beat the eggs in a bowl with the cheese and plenty of pepper until thoroughly combined.

4 When the pasta is cooked, drain and return it to the pan but don't return the pan to the heat.

5 Pour over the eggs and cheese and add the pancetta. Immediately stir everything together so that the eggs scramble lightly and pull the dish together. The fat from the pancetta should also sizzle and fry as it mingles with the pasta. Serve immediately.

pasta al sugo di funghi

PASTA WITH A MUSHROOM SAUCE

The flavor of the mushrooms is vital for the successful outcome of this dish. If the mushrooms have not got an intense taste of their own, the tomatoes and garlic will simply overwhelm any vestige of flavor that might exist. If using dried porcini, be sure to reserve the liquid and add it to the sauce.

Serves 4

10oz dried porcini or similar full-flavored mushrooms or fresh,
cleaned, and sliced porcini or similar
full-flavored mushrooms
3 large tablespoons olive oil
½ onion, chopped
2 garlic cloves, chopped fine
4 large fresh tomatoes, peeled and roughly chopped
or 6 canned plum tomatoes, drained and squeezed dry
2 tablespoons chopped fresh Italian parsley
14oz pasta, such as pappardelle, tagliatelle, or fettuccine
sea salt and freshly ground black pepper

TO SERVE
freshly grated Parmigiano Reggiano (optional)

1 If using dried porcini, soak in a bowl of hand-hot water for 20 minutes, then drain and reserve until required.

2 Heat the olive oil in a large saucepan. Add the onion and garlic and fry gently for about 8 minutes, stirring frequently. Add the tomatoes and stir thoroughly.

3 Add the mushrooms and season to taste. Stir gently and cook slowly for about 40 minutes, or until the sauce becomes creamy and the mushrooms are very soft. Sprinkle with the fresh parsley and stir through just before use.

4 Bring a large saucepan of salted water to a boil. Add the pasta, stir and return to a boil, and simmer until just al dente. Drain thoroughly and return to the pan.

5 Add the sauce and mix together, then transfer to a large platter or individual plates and serve immediately with freshly grated Parmigiano Reggiano if desired.

pasta alla norma

PASTA WITH NORMA SAUCE

O*ne of Sicily's very best recipes, which is as dramatic and exciting to look at as it is delicious to eat.*

∽

Serves 4

2 large, long eggplants, sliced lengthwise
1 onion, quartered
1 carrot
1 celery stalk
1 garlic clove
1lb ripe, juicy, sweet fresh tomatoes, or 2 cups premium canned tomatoes
2½ cups vegetable oil for deep-frying
14oz dried pasta, such as maccheroni, penne, or sedani
4 tablespoons rich, sweet extra virgin olive oil
about 12 small sprigs or large leaves of fresh basil
2 cups freshly grated salted ricotta or pecorino cheese
sea salt and freshly ground black pepper

1 Sprinkle the slices of eggplant with sea salt, then lay them in a wide colander. Cover tightly with a plate and place a weight on top of the plate. Stand the colander in the sink or over a basin for 1 hour to let the bitter juices of the eggplants drain away.

2 Meanwhile, make the tomato sauce. Place the onion, carrot, celery, garlic, and tomatoes in a heavy saucepan. Cover with a lid and place the vegetables over a low heat to cook in their own juices gently for about 40 minutes, or until all the vegetables are soft.

3 Push the softened vegetables though a food mill, or process in a food processor until puréed. Return the sauce to the heat to boil again until reduced to a thick texture.

4 Remove the saucepan from the heat, add salt and pepper to taste and reserve until required.

5 Rinse the eggplant slices and pat dry, then cut them into neat cubes.

6 Heat the vegetable oil in a large skillet until sizzling hot. Add the eggplant cubes and fry until soft and shiny. Drain the eggplant thoroughly on paper towels and keep warm.

7 Bring a large saucepan of salted water to a boil. Add the pasta, stir and return to a boil, and cook until al dente.

8 Reheat the tomato sauce gently and stir in the olive oil, then remove from the heat.

9 Drain the pasta and return it to the hot pan. Now you are ready to quickly assemble the dish.

10 Add a little amount of the tomato sauce to the pasta, just enough to coat it lightly. Arrange the pasta in a high mound on a warmed platter. Pour the remaining sauce over the top so that it trickles down. Arrange the hot fried eggplant cubes down the sides of the mound. Arrange the basil sprigs half buried in the tomato sauce, then sprinkle the top with the cheese and serve immediately.

1. You will need plenty of water for the pasta to move around freely while it cooks. Ideally you need 5 quarts of water to 2¼lb pasta. You should not need to add oil to the water to prevent the pasta from sticking, unless you do not have enough water in the pan or the pan is too small.

2. The required amount of salt is ½ tablespoon of salt per quart. This is dependent upon how savory your sauce or dressing is going to be. Always make sure you salt the water.

3. Don't even think about putting your pasta into the salted water until the water has achieved a rolling boil.

4. Drain the pasta as soon as it is cooked to the point when you as the cook feel it is ready—the only way to tell is to scoop a piece out and taste it.

5. Once drained, dress the pasta immediately and serve it as soon as possible.

Remember that the pasta continues to cook even out of the saucepan, so get yourself ready to drain, dress, and generally prepare it for the table while it is cooking. A little residual water is useful for loosening or diluting your sauce only in very rare circumstances. Usually it is preferable to thoroughly drain all the water from the pasta. If, however, the sauce is too thick and will not be easy to distribute through the freshly cooked pasta, then take a little water from the pan in which the pasta is cooking and gently stir it through the sauce to loosen it up slightly.

pasta al pesto alla genovese

PASTA WITH PESTO IN THE GENOVESE STYLE

Pesto is one of those Italian ingredients that has become part of the international pantry, along with balsamic vinegar, pasta, and a few others. Its origins lie deep in the heart of maritime Genova, and it was used as a condiment for one or two shapes of handmade pasta; either the curly little trofie pasta or the long flat ribbons called trenette. In either case, the traditional way of cooking and serving this dish is to cook one-third cubed boiled potatoes, one-third green beans, and one-third pasta, all dressed generously with pesto. Just as with so many of these recipes, there is no definitive formula. Each household, restaurant, and Mama will insist that theirs is the ultimate and only recipe. The recipe given here is my own version and I hope you will feel free to increase or decrease the quantities as you work, tasting and adjusting as you feel. This is necessary, because in my experience no two basil plants are ever quite the same, and it is basil which is the fundamental ingredient in pesto.

Serves 4

PESTO ALLA GENOVESE
2 or 3 or 4 large handfuls fresh basil leaves
a pinch of rock salt
2 or 3 garlic cloves, halved
a handful of pine nuts
2 to 6 tablespoons grated Parmigiano Reggiano, pecorino,
or half and half cheese
about ¼ cup best quality olive oil
sea salt and freshly ground black pepper

TO SERVE
6oz fresh green beans, boiled or steamed until tender
6oz potatoes, peeled, cubed, and boiled or steamed until tender
8oz Trofie or other type of small curly or narrow ribbon pasta

1 Place the basil, salt, and garlic into a food processor and whiz to a smooth green purée. Alternatively, use a mortar and pestle.

2 Add the pine nuts and cheese and process briefly. Begin to add the oil a little at a time, until you have reached a smooth, creamy texture. Season with salt and pepper to taste and use as required.

3 Meanwhile, bring a large saucepan of salted water to a boil. Add the pasta, return to a boil, and cook until the pasta is al dente. Minutes before the end of cooking add the cooked beans and potatoes to heat them through.

4 Drain the pasta and vegetables and return to the pan, reserving a little water from the pasta pan. Dress with the pesto, which is slightly diluted with a little of the reserved water from the pasta pan to help it coat all the other ingredients.

5 Serve immediately. It is not usual to serve extra Parmigiano Reggiano at the table when eating pesto.

NOTE ~ If you are using a pestle and mortar, remember to press the basil leaves against the sides: do not bang downwards with the pestle otherwise the basil leaves will be bruised.

If using a food processor, remember to taste as you go along and adjust the quantities according to personal preference.

ravioli di ricotta e spinaci

RICOTTA AND SPINACH RAVIOLI

The combination of ricotta with spinach is an absolute classic, enlivened by the addition of freshly grated nutmeg. You can make these into rectangular shapes, as explained in the recipe, or crescent shaped or even triangular. To cut down on the overall amount of work, you could simply make them extra big, so you need to make only two to eight per person. In this case, be sure the pasta is rolled out extra thin. Any leftover pasta can be cut into other shapes, and the filling can be used to dress the pasta like a sauce, slackened first with a ladleful of boiling water from the pasta pan.

Serves 4

2¼lb fresh spinach, steamed, drained, and chopped
1 tablespoon unsalted butter
a large pinch of grated nutmeg
6oz fresh ricotta
⅔ cup freshly grated Parmigiano Reggiano
1 egg yolk, beaten
sea salt and freshly ground black pepper

PASTA
3 cups all-purpose flour
3 eggs

DRESSING
6 tablespoons sunflower oil
a large handful of fresh sage leaves
⅔ cup unsalted butter, melted
1 cup freshly grated Parmigiano Reggiano

1 To make the filling, place the chopped, cooked spinach in a saucepan with the butter and heat through for a few minutes, stirring constantly. Add salt, pepper, and nutmeg to taste.

2 Transfer to a bowl and add the ricotta. Mix together thoroughly and adjust the seasoning if necessary. Mix in the grated Parmigiano Reggiano and the beaten egg. Cover and reserve until required.

3 Make the pasta according to the recipe on page 116 and cut into long wide strips. Dot the filling along one strip, leaving a good space between each mound of filling. Lay another strip of pasta on top and press round each mound of pasta with the sides of your hands.

4 Using a pastry wheel or sharp knife, cut into squares or circles, leaving a sensible edge around the filling so that it cannot escape during cooking and making sure there is no air trapped inside each sealed raviolo. You should end up with about 12 ravioli per person. Any leftover filling can be used as a dressing for freshly cooked hot pasta.

5 Heat the sunflower oil in a small skillet. Add the sage leaves and quickly fry until just crisp. Drain on paper towels, then reserve until required.

6 Bring a large saucepan of salted water to a boil. Keep a large serving bowl over a separate pan of simmering water close to the pan where you will cook the ravioli. Cook the ravioli in batches, removing them from the water when they are cooked with a slotted spoon.

7 Transfer the ravioli to the warmed bowl and coat generously with melted butter and a sprinkling of freshly grated Parmigiano Reggiano and the crumbled fried sage leaves. Continue in this way until all the ravioli are cooked and dressed. Serve immediately.

ripieno per tortellini

TORTELLINI FILLING

This is the traditional Bolognese meat filling for tortellini, ravioli, and many other types of filled pasta. The idea is that the filling should be incredibly flavorsome, so you only need to use a small quantity in order to taste all the different kinds of meat used in the filling.

Makes enough filling for tortellini for 10 people

2 tablespoons unsalted butter
4oz pork loin, cubed
2oz turkey breast, cubed
4oz prosciutto crudo, in one piece (preferably prosciutto di Parma)
4oz mortadella, in one piece
2 eggs, beaten
2⅓ cups freshly grated Parmigiano Reggiano
a large pinch of nutmeg
salt and freshly ground black pepper

TO SERVE
2 quantities of fresh pasta (see page 116)

1 Melt the butter in a large skillet. Add the pork and
turkey and fry for 10 minutes. Allow to cool slightly. Mince
them three times or process once in a food processor, together
with the prosciutto and mortadella.

2 Stir in the eggs, salt and pepper, Parmigiano Reggiano,
and nutmeg. Mix together thoroughly, then reserve
until required.

3 Use the mixture to fill the pasta (see below), using a very
small quantity so that the filled pasta does not burst in the
cooking process. Tortellini are traditionally cooked and served in
a rich poultry broth or boiled in salted water, drained, and served
smothered in a rich cream sauce.

TO MAKE THE TORTELLINI ~ Roll out a sheet of fresh pasta
as finely as you dare. Using a pastry wheel or sharp knife, cut
into small squares or circles and place ¼ teaspoon of filling in
the center. Fold the pasta in half, either into a triangle or a
semicircle and press the outer ends together firmly. Turn the
central section outward and downward, almost inside out.

la lasagna

LASAGNA

The amount of work required to make a real lasagna is quite immense. There is a lot of preparation involved in making up all the different elements before you get to the point of assembly. The real traditional recipe from Ferrara uses far more ingredients, including pancetta, prosciutto, pork loin, chicken livers, truffles, and cream, not to mention peas! Here is my toned down version of that recipe, which I feel is somewhat more accessible to most. In any case, Italians choose to make lasagna for special occasions, given the labor of love involved.

Serves 6

PASTA
5 cups all-purpose flour
6 large eggs
or
1¼ cups ready-made dried lasagne

FILLING
2 tablespoons olive oil
1 large onion, chopped fine
1 large carrot, chopped fine
1 large celery stalk, chopped fine
1lb fresh lean ground beef or veal
½ cup dry red wine
2 cups strained canned tomatoes
a handful of dried porcini mushrooms, soaked in warm water
for at least 1 hour
sea salt and freshly ground black pepper

BÉCHAMEL SAUCE
3 tablespoons unsalted butter
4 tablespoons all-purpose flour
2½ cups milk
a pinch of freshly grated nutmeg
4oz mozzarella, cubed
1 cup freshly grated Parmigiano Reggiano

1 Make the fresh pasta according to the recipe on page 116. Roll out the dough until paper thin, then cut into rectangles about the size of your palm.

2 Bring a large saucepan of salted water to a boil. Add the pasta in batches of about three at a time and cook briefly. As soon as the pasta rises to the surface of the water, slip it out with a slotted spoon and lay it carefully on a wet, clean cloth.

3 Keep the cooked pasta moist under wet cloths until required for assembling the dish.

4 Make the filling. Heat the oil in a large skillet. Add the onion, carrot, and celery and fry together for about 10 minutes, then add the ground meat and fry gently until the meat is well browned.

5 Add the wine and boil quickly for 2 minutes, then pour in the tomatoes and stir thoroughly. Return to a boil, then reduce the heat to a low simmer and leave to cook slowly, stirring frequently, for about 90 minutes. Drain the dried porcini mushrooms and roughly chop. Reserve the mushroom soaking water, add the mushrooms to the sauce, and stir.

6 Strain the water in which the mushrooms were soaked through a double layer of paper towels or cheesecloth, then add this to the sauce. Season to taste, stir, and let simmer for an additional 1 hour.

7 Prepare the béchamel sauce by melting the butter in a saucepan. Add the flour and mix together until a yellow paste

is formed. Pour in all the milk and beat to prevent lumps forming. Add salt and nutmeg to taste and simmer gently for about 15 minutes, stirring constantly. When the sauce is thick enough to coat the back of a spoon, remove it from the heat and cover the surface with a little cold water to prevent a skin from forming. Reserve until required. As soon as the tomato sauce is ready, you can begin to assemble the dish.

8 Preheat the oven to 400°F. Cover the base of a large baking dish with a thin layer of béchamel sauce, then cover with a layer of pasta sheets, then a layer of tomato sauce, a sprinkling of mozzarella cubes and some of freshly grated Parmigiano Reggiano, and finally another layer of béchamel sauce. Continue until you have used up all the ingredients, ending with a layer of Besciamella and a final sprinkling of Parmigiano Reggiano.

9 Allow to stand for about 10 minutes before baking in the oven for 30 minutes. When the lasagna comes out of the oven, allow it to stand for at least 5 minutes before cutting it into portions.

NOTE ~ You could be making your fresh pasta while your tomato sauce is simmering if you want to save time.

gnocchi al pomodoro

GNOCCHI WITH TOMATO SAUCE

*G*nocchi made as rubbery and hard as small balls, are *really quite easy to make. The skill and the difficulty is to make them as light as a feather, so that they almost hover on the plate, almost levitating! If this sounds a little off-putting, it is not what I mean. What I really mean is that gnocchi take practice and you need to experiment two or three times before you achieve anything like the desired effect, so don't be too frustrated or disappointed if they don't quite work out the first time!*

Serves 6

2¼lb floury potatoes, scrubbed
3 eggs, beaten
3 cups all-purpose flour or less, depending upon the texture
of the potatoes
salt
ready-made tomato sauce (see page 124), use enough to just
coat the gnocchi

TO SERVE
freshly grated Parmigiano Reggiano

1 Boil the potatoes until soft, drain and peel quickly, then press through a potato ricer twice.

2 Blend in the eggs and flour in a large bowl or directly on a clean countertop. Add as little flour as you can get away with, testing the texture as you go along by seeing if the dough can hold the gnocchi shape without melting into goo. Work carefully and quickly, because the more you handle the dough, the harder and bouncier it will become!

3 Make a soft dough with your hands, then roll it into long thumb thick cylinders. Cut into sections and form into small concave gnocchi shapes, pressing them against the back of a fork. Spread them out on a large board and reserve until required.

4 Bring a large saucepan of salted water to a boil. Drop in the gnocchi and leave them to cook until they float on the surface. Scoop them out with a slotted spoon and arrange them in a well-greased ovenproof dish. You need about 12 gnocchi per person.

5 Pour over a rich tomato sauce and serve immediately with freshly grated Parmigiano Reggiano.

gnocchi alla romana

SEMOLINA GNOCCHI

*O*f all the various gnocchi recipes, this is the easiest to
make as the gnocchi are simply cut out in disks rather
than having to be shaped into their traditional curled and
ribbed form. You can make this recipe more piquant by adding
some thin slices of Gorgonzola between the layers.

Serves 6

4 cups milk
1⅔ cups semolina
2 egg yolks
1⅓ cups freshly grated Parmigiano Reggiano
4 tablespoons unsalted butter
a pinch of ground nutmeg
sea salt and freshly ground black pepper

1 Preheat the oven to 425°F. Bring the milk to a boil in a large saucepan. Sprinkle in the semolina with one hand so that it falls like rain into the water and beat constantly with the other.

2 Beat constantly to prevent lumps forming. Continue until the mixture begins to thicken, then use a wooden spoon to stir constantly for about 10 minutes as the mixture thickens. You know it is ready when it begins to come away from the sides and base of the pan and forms a rounded, soft ball.

3 Remove the pan from the heat. Stir in the egg yolks, half the cheese and half the butter. Season with the nutmeg, salt, and pepper to taste.

4 Dampen the countertop lightly with cold water and tip out the semolina mixture. Spread it out flat with a spatula dipped in cold water to a thickness of about ½in. Using a pastry cutter or an upturned tumbler, cut all the semolina into even-sized rounds.

5 Use some of the remaining butter to grease a shallow, ovenproof dish. Arrange a layer of scraps from the cut out semolina rounds on the base of the dish. Cover with a little grated Parmigiano Reggiano and a few dots of butter.

6 Cover with a layer of slightly overlapping semolina rounds, and cover these with cheese and butter as before. Repeat until all the ingredients have been used up.

7 Melt any remaining butter and trickle it over the top. Bake in the oven for about 15 minutes before serving.

NOTE ~ It is a good idea to test the mixture when making potato gnocchi before shaping them all. To do this, when the dough feels about right, roll out a small piece and cut into sections. Shape into their traditional form and drop them into a small pan of boiling water. Using a slotted spoon, scoop out four or five of these gnocchi as soon as they float to the surface and let them fall on to a plate. Taste them, checking for seasoning and texture. If they need adjusting, by the addition of more salt, extra egg, or flour, you will still be in time to do so. Test again, in the same way, before finally deciding you are happy enough with the result to continue with the rest of the dough.

polenta con salsicce e fagioli

POLENTA WITH SAUSAGE AND BEANS

Polenta is one of those Italian staples from the cold northern regions of the country, which has never become as popular, outside of the areas of its origin, as other Italian specialties. Made with cornmeal, trickled into boiling salted water and stirred until thick and cooked through, the resulting, very thick porridge is then cut into slabs or poured into a bowl and served alongside a stew or with cheese, fish, or vegetables. It is very much a dish that belongs to the country's poorer past when bread and meat were rare. Traditionally wet polenta would be poured onto a board in the center of a table and everyone would dive in and help themselves—real rustic eating! This classic combination of hot polenta served in slabs with beans and sausages simmered together like a casserole would have kept both hunger and cold at bay for many households during the course of Italy's checkered past.

2½ cups fresh or dried or canned cranberry beans
2 tablespoons olive oil
2 garlic cloves, chopped
1 onion, chopped
1 celery stalk, chopped
1 carrot, chopped
2 teaspoons chopped fresh parsley
1 tablespoon tomato paste, diluted in 4 tablespoons warm water
12 Italian sausages
sea salt and freshly ground black pepper

POLENTA
7 cups cold water
1½ cups ground cornmeal (polenta flour)

1 If using fresh or dried beans, soak overnight in cold water, then drain and rinse. Boil quickly in salted water for 5 minutes to remove the natural toxins, then drain and rinse again. Cover generously with fresh water and simmer gently for about 40 minutes, or until tender. If using canned beans, rinse under cold running water.

2 Heat the olive oil in a large saucepan. Add the garlic, onion, celery, carrot, and parsley and fry until all the vegetables are soft, then add the tomato paste. Stir together thoroughly and add the sausages. Fry for a few minutes, then add the beans and all

their liquid. Canned beans can be added at this stage with extra water or stock added to make up the liquid required.

3 Add salt and pepper to taste and cover with a lid. Leave to simmer for about 45 minutes, or until thickened and rich, with the consistency of a stew.

4 While the sausages and beans are simmering, prepare the polenta. Pour the water into a wide, heavy, preferably copper pan and place it over a high heat. Bring the water to a boil. Sprinkle in the cornmeal (polenta flour) with one hand and so that it falls like rain into the water and beat constantly with the other.

5 When all the cornmeal (polenta flour) has been beaten into the water, reduce the heat to medium low and begin to stir with a strong, long-handled wooden spoon until the polenta comes away from the sides of the pan. This will take about 45 minutes and requires a strong action.

6 Turn the polenta out onto a wooden board and smooth it into a mound shape with a spatula. Allow it to stand for about 5 minutes, then cut it into slabs and serve hot with its accompanying stew or casserole. Alternatively, serve with a slice of very strong flavored cheese such as Gorgonzola.

SERVING SUGGESTION ~ As an alternative, you can leave the polenta to go completely cold, then slice as required and broil, fry, or bake. Serve the sausages and beans poured over a wedge of the freshly sliced polenta.

risotto

risotto alla parmigiana

CHEESE AND BUTTER RISOTTO

This is the basic recipe, from which all other risotto variations are created. You can add other ingredients, such as vegetables, chicken livers, and herbs to this recipe. Making risotto successfully is all about texture, so it is important to master a simple version like this one before moving on to recipes which are more complicated because they contain lots of other ingredients. In this recipe, the only thing you need to concentrate on is the rice itself.

Serves 6

3 tablespoons unsalted butter
1 medium onion, chopped fine
2½ cups risotto rice
about 6 cups best quality simmering chicken or meat broth or
very strong flavored vegetable broth
6 tablespoons freshly grated Parmigiano Reggiano
sea salt and freshly ground black pepper

1 Melt half the butter in a large saucepan. Add the onion and fry for about 10 minutes over a very low heat, or until the onion is soft but not browned.

2 Stir in the rice and thoroughly toast the grains for about 5 minutes until they become opaque and coated in the butter.

3 Add the first 3 ladles of hot broth and stir. Reduce the heat to low and continue to stir the broth. Add one ladleful of broth at a time, letting the rice absorb the liquid before adding more hot broth.

4 When the rice is almost completely soft and creamy, stir in the cheese and the remaining butter. Taste and adjust seasoning if necessary, then cover and allow to rest for about 3 minutes before transferring to a platter to serve.

risotto ai quattro formaggi

RISOTTO WITH FOUR CHEESES

This plain and simple risotto has a stronger cheese base than the previous recipe. Again, it acts as a good starting point for a multitude of other risottos by adding ingredients to it to suit your personal taste.

Serves 4

3 tablespoons unsalted butter
1 small to medium onion, chopped fine
1¾ cups risotto rice, such as Vialone Nano rice
about 5 cups best quality simmering chicken or meat broth or very flavorsome vegetable broth
5 tablespoons freshly grated Grana Padano cheese
1½oz fontina cheese, finely cubed
1½oz Emmenthal cheese, finely cubed
1oz Gorgonzola or Dolcelatte cheese, cubed
sea salt and freshly ground black pepper

1 Melt half the butter in a pan over a low heat. Add the onion and fry gently for about 10 minutes, or until the onion is soft but not browned.

2 Stir in the rice and thoroughly toast the grains, so that they are opaque but not browned.

3 Add the first ladle of hot broth and stir until almost all of the liquid has been absorbed by the grains, then add another ladle of broth. Continue adding the broth, letting the rice absorb the liquid before adding the next.

4 When the rice is almost completely soft and creamy, stir in the cheese until melted, then stir in the remaining butter. Taste and adjust the seasoning as required, then cover and allow to rest for about 3 minutes before transferring to a platter to serve.

risi e bisi

VENETIAN RICE AND PEAS

This recipe is cooked in the traditional way of making risotto, without frying the rice in fat at the beginning of the recipe. The end result is more like a very thick soup rather than a risotto. Not all recipes call for pancetta, but in my opinion it adds flavor.

∽

Serves 4

2¼lb sweet tender young fresh peas or 4 cups frozen petit pois, thawed
2½ tablespoons extra virgin olive oil
2 tablespoons unsalted butter
½ mild, sweet onion, chopped fine
2oz pancetta, chopped
½ cup chopped fresh parsley
8 cups good-quality simmering beef, veal, vegetable, or chicken broth
1¾ cups risotto rice such as Vialone Nano Gigante
about 1 cup freshly grated Parmigiano Reggiano
sea salt and freshly ground black pepper

1 If you are using fresh peas, shell all the peas carefully and rinse them quickly in cold water.

2 Heat the olive oil and butter in a heavy pan. Add the onion and pancetta and fry for about 10 minutes. Add the parsley and stir. Fry gently for an additional 4 minutes. Add the peas and stir thoroughly.

3 Add just enough broth to barely cover and simmer very slowly until the peas become tender.

4 Add the rice, stir and add more broth. Season to taste and stir, waiting until the rice almost absorbs the broth before adding more. Continue in this way, adding broth and stirring, until the rice is cooked through.

5 When the rice is soft and tender, remove the pan from the heat, stir in the cheese and allow to rest for 3 minutes before transferring to a shallow bowl to serve with extra Parmigiano Reggiano.

NOTE ~ Bear in mind that this dish is always served much wetter than other risotti and should have a soupy texture.

risotto al tartufo

RISOTTO WITH TRUFFLE

I do appreciate that truffles are so expensive as to be out of reach for the majority of us, but should you ever stumble upon one or be given a truffle as a gift, this dish surely has to be one of the most delicious ways to enjoy it.

Serves 4

3 tablespoons unsalted butter
1 onion, chopped fine
1¾ cups carnaroli rice
1 large glass dry white wine
up to 8 cups simmering rich chicken broth
5 tablespoons freshly grated Grano Padano or Parmigiano
Reggiano
1 truffle (size is everything!), cleaned, brushed,
and ready to shave
sea salt and freshly ground black pepper

1   Melt half the butter in a large saucepan. Add the onion and fry gently until very soft but not browned.

2   Add all the rice and thoroughly toast the grains, stirring constantly, for about 5 minutes.

3   Add the wine and stir for 1 minute, then add 3 ladles of broth and stir it all together. Keep the heat low and continue to stir and add broth, one ladle at a time, waiting each time for the grains to absorb the liquid. Don't rush it!

4   As soon as the rice is cooked but neither chalky nor too soft, remove the pan from the heat and stir in the Parmigiano Reggiano and the remaining butter.

5   Stir, taste, and add salt and pepper as required. Cover and allow to rest for about 4 minutes, then stir again and transfer to 4 serving plates. Shave as much or as little of the truffle over the steaming risotto as you want to and indulge yourself!

NOTE ~ White truffles are more rare and much more expensive than the black. I can't tell you why, you'll have to find out for yourself and the only way to do that is to try them both! I am not a fan of using truffle oil as an alternative to real truffles, as I don't think much real truffle is involved.

risotto al vino rosso

RED WINE RISOTTO

*A*lthough this risotto is delicious, the color is often
off-putting, which is as unfortunate as it is unavoidable!
*Use a bottle of wine that is as good as possible to make up for
the appearance of your finished dish.*

Serves 4

3 tablespoons unsalted butter
1 red onion, chopped fine
½ celery stalk, chopped very fine
3 fresh sage leaves, chopped fine
2 cups risotto rice, such as Vialone Nano or arborio rice
1 bottle full-bodied red wine
about 2 cups simmering beef, chicken or vegetable broth
⅔cup freshly grated Parmigiano Reggiano
sea salt and freshly ground black pepper

1 Melt half the butter in a large saucepan. Add the red onion, celery, and sage and fry until the onion and celery are soft and translucent.

2 Add the rice and stir until the grains are toasted, opaque, and crackling hot. Do not let the rice or the vegetables brown during this process.

3 Add the first glass of red wine. Stir until the wine has been absorbed and the acid from the alcohol has evaporated, then add more wine. Continue until all the wine has been used.

4 At this point, begin adding the hot broth one ladleful at a time, stirring constantly and allowing the liquid to be absorbed before adding more.

5 When the rice is creamy and velvety, but still firm to the bite, remove the pan from the heat and stir in the remaining butter and the cheese. Taste and adjust the seasoning as required and cover.

6 Allow to stand for about 3 minutes, stir one last time and then transfer to a warmed platter to serve.

risotto alla primavera

SPRING VEGETABLE RISOTTO

This risotto depends upon the quality of the vegetables used in order to deliver the delicious, fresh, light taste which is so typical of this dish. Make sure you use tender, sweet vegetables that are packed with flavor. All the vegetables need to be chopped to about the same size as the peas.

Serves 6

4 tablespoons unsalted butter
2 plump scallions, chopped fine
a handful of fine green beans, trimmed
3 baby carrots, roughly chopped
3 young, tender zucchini, with their flowers if possible, roughly chopped
3 to 4 tablespoons fresh peas, podded
12 young asparagus spears
3 very small florets fresh sprouting broccoli, roughly chopped
2½ cups carnaroli rice
¼ cup dry white wine
6 cups simmering vegetable or light chicken broth
3 heaping tablespoons freshly grated Grana Padano cheese
sea salt and freshly ground pepper

1 Melt half the butter in a large saucepan. Add the vegetables and gently fry for about 8 to 10 minutes. Add the rice and stir to coat with the butter and vegetables.

2 Add the wine and stir for 1 minute to evaporate the alcohol. Begin to add the hot broth one ladleful at a time, stirring constantly and allowing the liquid to be absorbed before adding more. The rice will take 20 minutes to cook from the time you begin adding the liquid.

3 When the rice is creamy but is still firm to the bite, remove the pan from the heat. Taste and adjust the seasoning as required, then stir in the remaining butter and the freshly grated cheese.

4 Cover and allow to rest for 2 minutes, then stir again and transfer to a warmed platter to serve immediately.

NOTE ~ You may not need all the liquid, depending on the quality of the rice.

risotto con i funghi

MUSHROOM RISOTTO

Everybody's favourite risotto! A thousand versions of this recipe exist, but this one works for me every time! The more interesting the mushrooms, the tastier the final result will be. Always make sure wild mushrooms are safe to eat before cooking them. If in doubt—don't eat them! If using dried mushrooms, they will need to be soaked in hand hot water for a least 1 hour before using, and don't forget to strain and use the liquid in which they were soaked.

Serves 6

½lb mixed wild mushrooms
4 tablespoons unsalted butter
1 medium onion, chopped
1 garlic clove, chopped
1 small fresh rosemary sprig, chopped
1 large glass dry white wine
2½ cups arborio rice
6 cups simmering chicken or vegetable broth
sea salt and freshly ground black pepper

TO SERVE
freshly grated Parmigiano Reggiano (optional)

1 Pick over the mushrooms carefully, making sure they are clean and free of any forest debris, then clean thoroughly and roughly chop.

2 Place the onion, garlic, and rosemary in a large, heavy pan and fry gently.

3 Add the chopped mushrooms and stir together thoroughly. Cook the mushrooms until just soft.

4 Add the white wine and stir for 1 minute to evaporate the alcohol. Add the rice and salt and pepper to taste and stir until the grains are toasted. Begin to add the hot broth one ladleful at a time, stirring constantly and allowing the liquid to be absorbed before adding more.

5 When the rice is creamy but still firm to the bite, remove the pan from the heat. Stir in the remaining butter and cover.

6 Allow to stand for about 3 minutes before transferring to a warmed platter and serving. You may offer Parmigiano Reggiano separately, but if the mushrooms are really full of flavor, the extra cheese is probably superfluous.

NOTE ~ Please be very careful if you gather your own wild mushrooms. Make sure they are all edible and suitable for cooking with wine as some varieties become toxic when combined with alcohol. Several very good books exist to help you identify wild mushrooms safely.

risotto ai frutti di mare

RISOTTO WITH MIXED SEAFOOD

F eel free to vary the selection of seafood according to what
you find and what looks fresh and best at the time.
This is just a selection of possibilities, don't worry if you have to
leave something out or swap it for a different fish or shellfish.

∽∽

Serves 4 to 6

1 bottle dry white wine
1lb fresh baby clams (vongole), scrubbed clean
1lb fresh mussels, scrubbed and beards removed
⅔ cup extra virgin olive oil
½lb white fish fillet
½lb raw shrimp, shell on
6 cups simmering strong fish broth
½lb crayfish, shell on
1 crab, cooked and split open
½ dried red chile, chopped fine
3 garlic cloves, chopped fine
3 tablespoons chopped fresh parsley
2½ cups carnaroli rice
sea salt and freshly ground black pepper

1 Pour a glass of white wine into a deep skillet. Add the baby clams and steam well until all the shells have opened. Remove and discard any shells that do not open.

2 Remove three quarters of the clams from their shells and reserve, together with the ones still in their shells. Strain the juices from the skillet through a fine strainer into a bowl.

3 Cook the mussels in the same way as the clams and add their liquid to the bowl.

4 Heat 2 tablespoons of olive oil in a skillet. Add the fish fillet and fry on both sides, basting with the wine to keep it very soft. Season with salt and pepper to taste and flake it roughly. Remove from the heat and reserve until required.

5 Heat 3 tablespoons of olive oil in a separate skillet. Add the shrimp and quickly fry until they are bright pink and cooked through, turning frequently and basting with wine.

6 Peel the shrimp and add the shells and heads to the simmering fish broth.

7 Heat 3 tablespoons of olive oil in a skillet. Add the crayfish and quickly fry until cooked through, turning frequently and basting with wine. Once cooked, remove them from the pan and take off the legs and claws.

8 Cut open the tails and remove all the white flesh. Place the claws, legs, and reserved flesh with the peeled shrimp and reserve. Add the carcasses to the stock.

9 Remove all the dark and white meat from the crab, taking care to leave all the inedible parts behind. Reserve the claws.

10 Heat the remaining olive oil in a skillet. Add the chile, garlic, and parsley and fry for 2 minutes, then add the rice. Stir until the rice is thoroughly coated and crackling hot, then add a glass of wine.

11 Stir for 2 minutes to evaporate the alcohol, then add the juices from the clams and mussels. Stir until the grains absorb this liquid, then begin to alternate additions of wine and hot broth, which will need to be strained into the risotto. When the wine has been used, continue with the broth.

12 Continue until the risotto is about two-thirds cooked, then add all the cooked seafood and fish including the shells, legs, and claws. Stir together thoroughly and continue to cook as before, adding the fish broth gradually and stirring constantly.

13 When the rice is creamy but still firm to the bite, transfer to a warmed platter and arrange so that all the claws and shells are on the top. Serve immediately.

NOTE ~ All the raw seafood must be cooked separately, but all the liquid from the various seafood can be combined and used as part of the broth. Wash and clean everything really carefully.

risotto alla milanese
versione classica

CLASSIC MILANESE SAFFRON RISOTTO

This risotto is traditionally rich, so a green, fresh salad is always a good accompaniment. It also needs a light red wine such as a Valpolicella or a Bardolino. The saffron quantity is ultimately up to you and also dependent upon how strong your batch of saffron powder turns out to be. I usually add one sachet first, taste, and adjust as necessary.

Serves 6

4 tablespoons unsalted butter
½ onion, chopped fine
1½oz raw beef bone marrow, chopped
2½ cups risotto rice, such as Vialone Gigante
6 cups simmering rich broth traditionally made with veal or beef and assorted vegetables
1 to 3 sachets of saffron powder
⅔ cup freshly grated Parmigiano Reggiano

1 Melt half the butter in a large saucepan. Add the onion and beef marrow and fry very gently.

2 When the onion is completely soft, add the rice. Stir until the grains are thoroughly coated and are crackling hot but not browned.

3 Begin to add the hot broth, stirring constantly and allowing the liquid to be absorbed before adding more.

4 Continue to cook the rice in this way, making sure that the rice always absorbs the broth before you add more liquid.

5 About halfway through cooking add the saffron powder and stir thoroughly until evenly combined.

6 When the risotto is creamy and velvety, but the rice grains are still firm to the bite, remove the pan from the heat. Stir in the remaining butter and the cheese.

7 Cover and allow to rest for 2 minutes, then stir again and transfer to a warmed platter. Serve immediately with extra freshly grated Parmigiano Reggiano.

Risotto is the great rice specialty of Italy. It is a triumphant dish, a dish that should be adored and respected along with all the other great Italian specialties such as pasta, pizza, and ice cream. It has all the versatility of pasta, and yet it is all too often overlooked and ignored because for various reasons, many people seem to think it is difficult to make!

For Italians (especially northern Italians where the dish has its origins), risotto is such an essential part of the cuisine that over the decades since it became a part of their menu they have developed many rice varieties which are specifically grown in order to make the dish.

The most basic premise for anybody making risotto for the first time is that you cannot make it unless you begin with the correct rice. The most common of these is called arborio, which is the best all-rounder, but there are two others: Carnaroli and Vialone Nano. Carnaroli has the largest and fattest grain, which means the rice is less likely to overcook. It also keeps its shape better and generally gives very good results, especially if one has not cooked very many risotti before. In Italy, this rice is reserved for very special occasions as it is considered to be the most precious. Vialone Nano has the smallest and hardest grain. It takes longer to cook and is a slightly more difficult to use. It is the rice preferred and most used by Venetians.

Once you have the correct rice, the next thing you need is some really good broth, which must be delectable enough to sip from a cup. It is not enough to simply use a bouillon cube (although this is permissible in an emergency!), and in an ideal world fresh homemade stock is the best option.

However, real life being what it is, for all those who claim not to have time to make broth: freshly made broth is now widely available in a whole range of flavors. Seeing how easy and satisfying it is to make broth, I have always found this a little bit mystifying, but most ready-made broth I have tasted has been delicious.

Armed with these two basic ingredients, you are then ready to begin cooking this truly great dish. If you follow the recipe carefully, you will see that contrary to what you might think, risotto is very simple to make!

Making risotto is essentially a five step process:

1. Having softened the onion, garlic, shallot, or leek in the butter or oil, add the rice at once and toast it thoroughly to heat it through, but without browning anything.

2. When the rice is really hot, add the first ladleful of hot broth or a glass of wine.

3. Continue to add the broth gradually, as well as any other ingredients required by the specific recipe.

4. When the rice is cooked, take the pan off the heat, stir in the final few ingredients, cover, and let it rest for a few minutes.

5. After resting, the risotto is ready to serve.

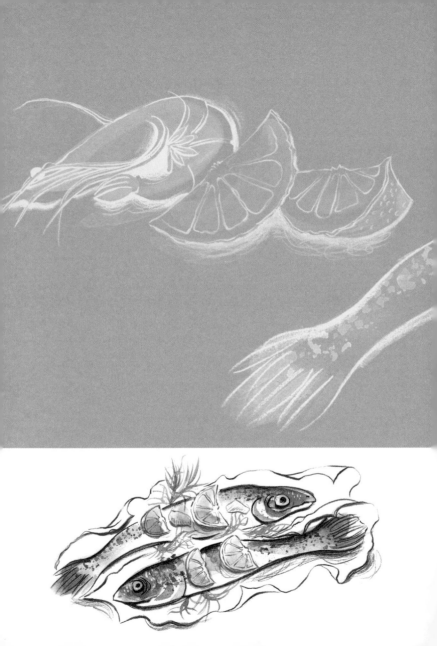

fish

zuppa di pesce

THICK AND CHUNKY FISH SOUP

This is the easiest recipe for making an authentic Italian tasting fish casserole. You can add mussels, shrimp, and other types of fish or seafood, although the basic recipe here calls only for filleted white fish, which makes it very easy to eat. The bread soaks up all the juices of the fish and is eaten at the end, once all the fish has gone.

Serves 6

about 3¼lb filleted fish of various kinds, such as cod, angler
fish, haddock, or flounder
8 tablespoons olive oil
5 garlic cloves, chopped fine
1 dried red chile
4 tablespoons chopped fresh parsley
3 handfuls cherry tomatoes, halved
½ cup dry white wine
about ¾ cup fish stock
12 thin slices ciabatta bread, toasted
1 garlic clove, peeled and left whole
salt and freshly ground black pepper

TO SERVE
2 tablespoons extra virgin olive oil
2 tablespoons chopped fresh Italian parsley

1 Prepare all the fish first. Trim it carefully, then wash and pat dry on paper towels.

2 Heat the olive oil in a deep pan. Add the garlic, chile, parsley, and tomatoes and cook for about 5 minutes. Add all the fish and stir. Season with salt and pepper and pour over the wine and stock. Cover and simmer gently for about 15 minutes.

3 Rub the toasted bread with the garlic and use the bread to line a large, wide bowl. Pour the hot fish casserole over the bread, drizzle with a little olive oil, sprinkle with the chopped Italian parsley and serve immediately.

pesce con i piselli

FISH WITH PEAS

This recipe basically combines fish with peas and turns into a type of casserole, moistened with wine and diluted tomato paste. You must use a firm fish, such as angler fish, for this dish so the flesh of the fish does not disintegrate. This recipe is often made using tender strips of pure white squid, which can stew away for ages without falling apart.

Serves 6

6 firm fish fillets, such as angler fish or hake
6 tablespoons olive oil
1 onion, chopped fine
1 large glass dry white wine
2 tablespoons chopped fresh parsley
5 cups fresh shelled peas or frozen peas
3 tablespoons tomato paste diluted in 1 cup hot water
sea salt and freshly ground black pepper

1 Trim and wash the fish fillets, pat dry on paper towels and reserve until required.

2 Heat the olive oil in a deep skillet. Add the onion and fry until the onion is transparent. Add the fish and fry until just browned on both sides, about 8 to 10 minutes.

3 Add the wine, and boil off the alcohol for 1 minute, then reduce the heat. Sprinkle with salt and pepper to taste, then sprinkle with the parsley.

4 Add the peas and the diluted tomato paste. Cover and allow to simmer for about 15 minutes, or until the peas are tender. Transfer to a warmed platter and serve immediately.

pesce arrosto

BAKED FISH ON A BED OF ROSEMARY POTATOES AND GARLIC

I really love this way of cooking fish. I can never decide which is more delicious, the potatoes or the fish itself! A bream, grouper, silver mullet, or other whole, firm fish is best, but any other kind of fish, filleted or whole, will also work quite well. You can add some thin slices of fennel to the potato base, or pile slices of thickly sliced red onion on top of the potatoes if you desire. If you have a handful of olives, you can also scatter them among the potatoes.

Serves 6

**1 whole fish such as porgy, grouper, trout or bream,
weighing about 3¼lb, gutted and scaled
6 medium potatoes, peeled and sliced to ½in thickness
8 tablespoons olive oil
4 garlic cloves, unpeeled and crushed
4 fresh rosemary sprigs
sea salt and freshly ground black pepper**

1 Preheat the oven to 375°F. Wash the fish thoroughly inside and out and pat dry on paper towels.

2 Place the potato slices in a large ovenproof dish and pour about three quarters of the olive oil over them. Season generously with salt and pepper and add the garlic and rosemary.

3 Toss the potatoes with the other ingredients until they are coated in the olive oil, garlic, and rosemary.

4 Rub the remaining olive oil over the fish, both inside and out, then season the fish with salt and pepper inside and out. Lay the fish on top of the potatoes.

5 Bake in the oven until the potatoes and the fish are cooked through, about 30 to 40 minutes. If necessary, baste the fish with a little water or dry white wine during the cooking process.

6 Transfer the fish to a flat platter and place the potatoes in a serving bowl, then serve.

NOTE ~ If you prefer, you can fillet the fish and lay the boneless fish on top of the sliced potatoes and other ingredients. In this case, the fish will cook more quickly, so the potatoes will need to be parboiled first, then drained and thinly sliced. Other vegetables might also need a little cooking before baking.

"One of the nicest things about life is the way we must regularly stop whatever it is we are doing and devote our attention to eating.

Luciano Pavaroti and William Wright, *Pavarotti, My Own Story*

pesce lesso

POACHED FISH

Pesce lesso is an Italian household stand-by for when one is feeling unwell or recovering from an illness. Light and tasty, it is important to take the time to prepare the stock in which you are going to poach the fish. Generally speaking, white fish such as cod, haddock, or whiting, or fish such as trout and salmon are best for poaching. Oily fish, such as sardines or mackerel, respond best to broiling or baking. You can also add a glass or two of dry white wine to the basic stock for extra flavor.

Serves 6

1 carrot, quartered
1 small onion or leek, quartered
1 celery stalk, quartered
5 fresh parsley sprigs
½ lemon
2 pinches of salt
6 black peppercorns
1 whole white fish or other fish suitable for poaching, such as
trout, weighing about 3½lb

TO SERVE
hollandaise sauce, mayonnaise, or lemon juice and olive oil

1 Place all the vegetables, the parsley, and lemon in a fish kettle or a large saucepan that is wide enough to take the length of the fish.

2 Cover generously with cold water. Add the salt and peppercorns. Cover, bring to a boil slowly and leave to simmer for about 20 minutes.

3 Clean, gut, and scale the trout. Wash thoroughly under cold running water, then place in the fish kettle or saucepan.

4 Cover and simmer slowly for about 10 minutes, then turn off the heat. Leave the fish in the fish kettle, covered with the lid, until the water is tepid.

5 Remove the fish carefully from the water, drain, and arrange in a dish. Serve warm or cold with hollandaise sauce, mayonnaise, or lemon juice and olive oil.

pesce nella crosta di sale

FISH BAKED IN SALT CRUST

The principle here is that the skin of the fish should be thick and resistant enough to not permit the salt to permeate the delicate meat under it. Be very careful to make sure that the skin of the fish is not pierced anywhere because if salt seeps through to the flesh it will spoil the taste. I have suggested grouper for this recipe, but any large, heavy scaled fish would be good—sea bream for instance.

Serves 6

1 fresh grouper, gutted, weighing about 3½ to 4lb (do not scale)
4 egg whites
3½lb finely ground coarse sea salt

TO SERVE
extra virgin olive oil
lemon wedges
freshly ground black pepper

1 Preheat the oven to 375°F. Wash the fish carefully inside and out and pat dry on paper towels. Lay it out in a baking dish lined with foil.

2 Beat the egg whites in a bowl until frothy, then carefully add all the salt, stirring. Cover the fish completely and very thickly with the egg white mixture. Bake in the oven for about 40 minutes.

3 When ready, the dish should look like a golden loaf of bread. Slide the fish off the foil with a spatula and onto a platter.

4 Break the salt crust at the table and serve carefully, lifting the fish out and placing on individual plates with a little drizzle of olive oil, a lemon wedge, and some black pepper.

NOTE ~ The cooking time for this recipe is largely a question of experience and guesswork, blended with instinct, as you can't pierce the salt crust to look at or feel the flesh of the fish without ruining everything with the salt!

triglie al vino bianco

RED MULLET WITH WHITE WINE

I just adore the combination of the flavor of the fish with the taste of the cured ham, as they seem to complement each other so perfectly. The origin of this dish is in the Marche, Rossini's region, where it is often enjoyed with a chilled bottle of Verdicchio dei Castelli di Jesi, the most famous of the superb white wines of this area.

Serves 4

8 red mullet fillets
8 slices Parma ham or prosciutto
3 tablespoons extra virgin olive oil
2 garlic cloves, crushed
3 fresh sage leaves, rubbed
¾ cup dry white wine
sea salt and freshly ground black pepper

1 Wash the fish fillets and pat dry on paper towels. Wrap the fish fillets in the ham.

2 Heat the olive oil in a wide skillet. Lay the ham-wrapped fish in the skillet and cook gently on both sides for about 4 minutes. Turn once.

3 As the fish cooks, baste with the wine and add the garlic and sage. After 8 minutes, remove the fish from the skillet and season with salt and pepper to taste.

4 Add the remaining wine to the skillet and increase the heat. Bubble and stir for about 3 minutes, then allow to reduce until thickened. Pour over the fish and serve immediately.

sgombri al vino bianco e pomodoro

MACKEREL WITH WHITE WINE AND TOMATOES

The humble mackerel is an extremely delicious and sadly underrated fish. In this recipe, it is baked with garlic, white wine, and tomatoes, which lifts the fish out of its Atlantic image and turns it into a dish with a strong Mediterranean flavor. Any oily or white fish works very well cooked in this way, generically known, with a few variations to the basic format of the recipe as all'Isolana.

Serves 6

6 large or 12 smaller mackerel, heads and all bones removed
6 tablespoons olive oil
4 garlic cloves, sliced
a handful of black olives, stoned
2 tablespoons salted capers, rinsed
chopped peel of 1 lemon
butter, for greasing
¾ cup dry white wine
8 ripe tomatoes, peeled, seeded, and roughly chopped
1 heaping teaspoon dried oregano
salt and freshly ground black pepper

1 Preheat the oven to 375°F. Wash the mackerel and pat dry on paper towels. Oil them inside and out lightly, then place a few slices of garlic, olives, capers, and pieces of lemon peel inside each fish. Season inside and out.

2 Grease an ovenproof dish and arrange the mackerel in the dish side by side and head to tail. Sprinkle with a little more olive oil, and the remaining garlic, olives, capers, and lemon peel.

3 Pour over about half the wine. Cover with the tomatoes and sprinkle with the oregano. Place in the oven for 15 minutes, then remove the dish and add the remaining wine.

4 Return to the oven and bake for an additional 5 to 10 minutes until the fish is cooked through.

5 Remove the dish from the oven and sprinkle with the remaining olive oil just before serving.

VARIATION ~ The same combination of ingredients can be used to cook other fish fillets or even shrimp, and I have even used it to prepare mussels with great success.

tonno alla stemperata

TUNA STEAK WITH SICILIAN SAUCE

Tuna steaks are an integral part of the culinary scene in Sicily and this delicious sweet and sour sauce helps to bring out the flavor not only of the fish, but somehow of Sicily itself!

Serves 6

6 tuna steaks, weighing about 2¼lb in total
extra virgin olive oil
4 garlic cloves, minced
4 celery stalks, chopped
4 tablespoons pitted green olives
2 tablespoons capers, rinsed
4 tablespoons golden raisins, plumped in hot water for about
12 minutes, then drained
3 tablespoons white wine vinegar
1 heaping tablespoon fresh mint leaves, chopped fine
sea salt and freshly ground black pepper

1 Preheat the broiler or light a barbecue. Brush the tuna generously with olive oil on both sides, then broil the tuna over a medium-hot broiler or over a barbecue on both sides until browned on the outside and still pink in the middle.

2 Meanwhile, heat about 4 tablespoons of olive oil in a small saucepan. Add the garlic and celery and fry gently until the garlic and celery have softened.

3 Add the olives, capers, and golden raisins, and cook over a low heat for 2 to 3 minutes.

4 Add the vinegar and cook over a high heat for two to three minutes to evaporate the fumes of the vinegar. Season with salt and pepper to taste and add the chopped mint.

5 Arrange the cooked tuna on a platter, pour over the sauce and serve immediately.

NOTE ~ **How long the tuna takes to cook will depend upon the thickness of the steaks—but be careful not to overcook the fish or it will dry out and lose both flavor and texture.**

seppie in umido

SQUID CASSEROLE WITH SPICES

*A*dd some new potatoes or slices of old potatoes to the stew for the last 30 minutes of cooking to add bulk and make the dish more substantial. In Venice, it would be served with polenta. I first discovered this dish when making my original television series in Britain in 1989. Over the years I have gradually adapted it and made it my own, but it is still a great favorite and a happy way to remember those heady days!

Serves 6

4 tablespoons sunflower oil
1 large onion, chopped
2 garlic cloves, chopped
1 fresh rosemary sprig, leaves removed and chopped fine
2¼lb squid, cleaned and sliced
2 cups cold water
1¾ cups canned tomatoes, seeded and chopped
2 teaspoons tomato paste
a pinch of ground cinnamon
a pinch of freshly grated nutmeg
a pinch of ground ginger
sea salt and freshly ground black pepper

1 Heat the sunflower oil in a large saucepan. Add the onion and garlic and fry until soft and blond. Add the rosemary, then the squid. Mix together and cover with the cold water.

2 Bring to a boil, then cover, reduce the heat and allow to simmer for 45 minutes.

3 Add the tomatoes, tomato paste, salt, pepper, and all three of the spices.

4 Cover and simmer slowly for an additional 45 minutes, or until the squid is tender and the sauce has thickened. Serve hot or at room temperature.

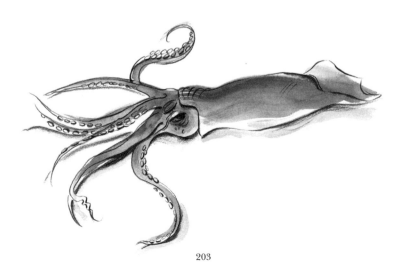

fritto di mare

MIXED FRIED SEAFOOD

For this remarkably simple and delicious fish dish you will require impeccably fresh fish. Traditionally, shrimp, squid rings, smelt and other small fish are used, but you can vary this if you wish. Don't flour the fish too soon before the oil is ready, or the flour will go tacky and make the fish terribly soggy. It is a good idea, when making fritto misto, to work in a well-ventilated position!

Serves 4

about 2¼lb mixed small fish including squid rings and shrimp
6 tablespoons all-purpose flour
sunflower oil, for deep-frying
sea salt

lemon wedges

1 Wash and prepare all the fish thoroughly and dry it very carefully on paper towels. Spread out the flour on a large plate, add the fish, and toss in enough flour to coat it lightly, shaking off any excess.

2 Heat the sunflower oil in a large, deep saucepan until a small piece of bread dropped into it sizzles instantaneously.

3 Deep-fry the fish quickly, in batches, until just golden and crisp. Drain well on plenty of paper towels and sprinkle with salt.

4 Serve piping hot and crisp, with lemon wedges to squeeze on the fish.

zuppa di cozze

MUSSEL SOUP

Nothing beats a morning clambering around on the rocks, finding mussels and bringing them home for lunch. Then sitting and cleaning them over a bucket with barnacles flying in all directions and those annoying little beards resisting your hardest efforts at tugging! I once spent a summer in the Outer Hebrides, where the mussels were so plentiful we could eat them every day. As with all seafood, please NEVER eat a mussel that needs forcing open.

Serves 4

3½lb fresh mussels, scrubbed and beards removed
3 tablespoons extra virgin olive oil
2 or 3 garlic cloves, unpeeled and lightly crushed
a handful of chopped fresh Italian parsley
2 tablespoons puréed tomatoes
1 cup dry white wine
8 slices ciabatta bread, lightly toasted and rubbed with
a peeled garlic clove
extra virgin olive oil, for drizzling
salt and freshly ground black pepper

1 Discard any mussels that remain closed. Place all the mussels in a wide skillet with no liquid at all and place them over a medium heat. Cover the skillet with a lid and shake to help the mussels to open.

2 Once all the mussels are open, remove them from the skillet and strain their liquor into a bowl. Reserve the liquor and discard all the mussels that remain closed. Reserve the remaining mussels until required.

3 Heat the olive oil in the same skillet. Add the garlic and fry for about 5 minutes. Add the parsley and puréed tomatoes, season to taste, and stir thoroughly.

4 Add the reserved mussels and wine and mix together thoroughly. Cook over a high heat for about 4 minutes, then remove the skillet from the heat.

5 Arrange the toasted garlic bread in the base of a wide bowl. Drizzle a thin stream of olive oil over the bread slices, then pour the mussels and all the liquid over the bread.

6 Serve immediately, remembering to place an empty bowl in the middle of the table for the empty mussel shells.

Wandering around an Italian market, anywhere near the sea is a wonderful experience for anybody who really enjoys fish. The range of different varieties is positively extraordinary, and it is usually possible to engage the vendors in all kinds of conversations of how best to prepare this or that fish in order to show it off to its very best advantage.

Sadly, for many people I meet this seems to be all they are prepared to do. They seem to find the idea of cooking fish or shellfish a very daunting prospect and one that they are simply not prepared to take on.

When asked why, one of the main reasons they give is to do with the smell of fish and the worry that an unpleasant smell will somehow pervade the house and they won't be able to get rid of it. In actual fact, fresh fish, and really there is no point in even considering the idea of cooking fish which is not absolutely fresh, does not have an unpleasant smell. Fresh fish should smell of the clean sea it came from and nothing else.

When selecting to buy, one should look for fish that still has a twinkle in the eye, whose scales and skin are sparkling and shiny, and whose gills are brilliantly rosy. The flesh should also feel firm to the touch. Sometimes the fish has gone into rigor, meaning that instead of lying flat, it is somehow still bent by movement, but all of this is meaningless if the fish smells. Whatever cosmetic cover up or improvements might have been adopted as sales measures by enthusiastic fish merchants the smell is what always gives the game away. Cartilaginous fish, in particular, begin to break down very quickly. If not absolutely fresh the smell of ammonia that comes from skate wings or a shark steak is unmistakable and very much the sort of experience that can put people off eating fish forever! Yet the truth is that eating fresh fish is very good for our basic health, and that cooking it is really easy.

My childhood memories of fishing trips will live with me forever. We would often drop nets in Italy at sunset, leaving the horseshoe shape swaying with the waves, safely anchored at each extremity by flagged buoys. At dawn, we'd be on the beach again, dragging the nets in onto the back of the boat, hand over hand. On the shoreline, as dawn turned the sea to an intense mother of pearl shimmer, we would each sit with our respective bucket, passing the net along and removing our catch. Each of us had to put their own specific bounty into their bucket. My duty was always to remove the squid, and my hands still bear the scars of many a squid's beak, which embedded itself in me as I struggled to free them without tearing a hole in the nets. Buckets suspended on handlebars, it was then time to pedal home for breakfast, with hopefully enough fish for everybody to enjoy for lunch.

poultry

petti di pollo ripieni

STUFFED CHICKEN BREAST

I like to vary this dish with different kinds of cheese or mozzarella, depending upon how strongly flavored I like it to be. Sometimes I add a simple tomato sauce either served separately in a sauce boat or poured over or around the finished dish just before serving.

Serves 6

4 plump chicken breasts, skinned and boned
12oz Fontina or Emmenthal cheese, sliced into strips
4 tablespoons olive oil
4 fresh sage leaves
sea salt and freshly ground black pepper

1 Using a sharp knife, trim the chicken breasts and make a long incision down the side of each one to create a pocket. Slip a few slices of the cheese inside each chicken breast and close the incision securely with toothpicks.

2 Heat the olive oil in a wide skillet. Add the sage and cook for about 5 minutes, then lay the chicken in the hot flavored oil and cook until sealed and browned on both sides.

3 When the chicken is golden brown, season with salt and pepper and turn the heat down low.

4 Cover and simmer very slowly for about 10 to 15 minutes, or until the chicken is thoroughly cooked through and the cheese has melted and is beginning to ooze out of the chicken. Transfer to a warmed platter, remove the toothpicks and serve.

spezzatino di pollo con funghi e pomodoro

CHICKEN CASSEROLE WITH MUSHROOM AND TOMATO

A very simple, classic way of making a chicken and mushroom casserole. I like to make the dish taste more interesting by adding some wild mushrooms to the mix.

Serves 4

1 x 3¼lb chicken, jointed into 6 pieces
4 tablespoons olive oil
2 garlic cloves, chopped fine
2 or 3 teaspoons fresh rosemary leaves
8oz fresh mushrooms, thickly sliced
1¼ cups puréed or canned chopped tomatoes
sea salt and freshly ground black pepper

1 Using a sharp knife, trim the chicken carefully. Heat the olive oil in a skillet. Add the garlic and rosemary and fry for about 4 minutes.

2 Lay the chicken in the pan and cook until sealed and browned on both sides. Add the mushrooms and mix together thoroughly.

3 Pour over the tomatoes and mix again. Season with salt and pepper to taste and cover.

4 Simmer gently for about 30 minutes, or until the chicken is thoroughly cooked through. Transfer to a warmed serving platter and serve immediately.

NOTE ~ You can add a glass of wine to the chicken at the very beginning, after browning, if you wish.

pollo ai peperoni

CHICKEN WITH PEPPERS

I adore this very typical home-cooked dish because it reminds me so much of those breathless, hot endless summers I spent as a child in Rome. The sweet taste of the peppers is so perfect with the chicken. All this dish needs are some boiled or steamed potatoes and a simple green vegetable such as green beans.

Serves 6

1 large chicken, or 2 smaller ones (about 5½ lb)
4 tablespoons olive oil
3 garlic cloves, sliced thin
½ cup dry white wine (traditionally Frascati), or more as required
4 juicy, thick red and yellow bell peppers, seeded
and sliced into strips
1lb fresh ripe tomatoes, peeled, seeded, and roughly chopped
or 1¾ cups canned chopped tomatoes
sea salt and freshly ground black pepper

TO SERVE
chopped fresh Italian parsley

1 Clean and trim the chicken, then joint it. Alternatively, buy chicken joints or buy whole chickens and ask the butcher to joint them for you.

2 Heat the olive oil in a wide, deep pan. Add the garlic and cook for about 5 minutes, then add the chicken joints. Brown the chicken all over, sprinkling with the wine.

3 Remove the chicken from the pan and reserve until required. Add the peppers and tomatoes to the pan and cook, stirring, for about 5 minutes.

4 Season with salt and pepper to taste and return the chicken to the pan. Stir again and cover. Simmer for about 40 minutes, or until the chicken is cooked through, basting occasionally with white wine or water.

5 Serve hot or cold, but not chilled, sprinkled with chopped Italian parsley.

pollo al forno

ITALIAN ROAST CHICKEN

The flavor of a chicken roasted in this way varies according to the herbs you want to add to the mixture. You can make it more or less pungent as you prefer, or according to what you serve alongside it. I always serve crisp, roasted potatoes with olive oil, lemon, and garlic. Superb either hot or cold, this has to be one of the most delicious ways to cook chicken joints to make a tasty, melting, juicy dish. If possible, use free-range chicken joints.

5 tablespoons olive oil
3 tablespoons fresh rosemary leaves or sage leaves, or fresh
marjoram or a combination of all three, chopped fine
4 garlic cloves, halved
1 large chicken, weighing about 4½lb, jointed
a little chicken broth, water, or dry white wine
sea salt and freshly ground black pepper

1 Preheat the oven to 400°F. Pour the olive oil into a large roasting pan and add the herbs and garlic. Add the chicken and mix it with the oil, turning the joints over to coat them thoroughly.

2 Season generously with salt and pepper, then roast in the oven for about 40 minutes, or until thoroughly cooked through, turning the joints over and basting occasionally with a little chicken broth, water, or wine. Serve hot or cold once crisp and golden brown.

VARIATION ~ I also cook rabbit, jointed in exactly the same way. Rabbit is much underrated and I believe should be more widely used. However, it does tend to dry out quite quickly, so do be sure to baste more frequently than if you were cooking chicken.

pollo alla diavola

DEVILED CHICKEN

This very traditional way of cooking a chicken could not be more simple, but the finished result is so delicious. It tastes best of all if eaten with your fingers, outdoors under a shady tree! You could also use poussins for this dish, calculating one poussin per person and reducing the cooking time as the poussins, being smaller, will take less time to cook.

Serves 6

2 oven-ready chickens, each one weighing about 1¾lb
about 6 tablespoons olive oil
sea salt and freshly ground black pepper

1 Cut open the chickens along the breastbone and flatten it as much as possible. You can ask the butcher to do this for you.

2 Preheat the broiler or light the barbecue. Press the open chicken hard downward and outward to make it as flat as possible, sometimes a clean brick is used to help keep the chicken as flat as possible against the grill.

3 Rub it all over with the olive oil, salt, and pepper. Grill them on both sides until thoroughly cooked through. You should end up with a very well browned, in fact very blackened exterior, and a well cooked but still juicy middle. Serve immediately, jointed.

spezzatino di pollo in bianco

LIGHT CHICKEN CASSEROLE

This is a very light dish, quick and easy to make without too many frills. I quite like the way the zucchini almost goes completely pulpy, forming a kind of sauce. Adapted from an original recipe by the famous Neapolitan chef Fabrizio Carola.

1¾lb lean chicken meat, boned and neatly cubed
½ cup extra virgin olive oil
1 tablespoon fresh rosemary leaves or 1 teaspoon
dried rosemary
4 garlic cloves, unpeeled
5 tablespoons dry white wine
4 medium parboiled potatoes, cubed
2 zucchini, cut into thick chunks
2 carrots, cut into small chunks
sea salt and freshly ground black pepper

TO SERVE
crisp, green salad

1 Preheat the oven to 350°F. Carefully trim all the chicken. Heat the olive oil in a large, flameproof casserole dish. Add the chicken and cook over a high heat, sprinkling it with the rosemary, garlic cloves, and salt and pepper until sealed and browned all over.

2 When the chicken is well browned, add the wine and cook for an additional 5 minutes, then add the potatoes, zucchini, carrots, and the remaining oil.

3 Stir well, then transfer the casserole dish to the oven and roast for about 30 minutes, or until the chicken and potatoes are brown and crisp on the outside. Serve immediately with a fresh green salad.

tacchina arrosto

ROAST STUFFED TURKEY

When it comes to cooking and serving turkey in Italy we tend to choose a smaller, succulent bird which will not dry out as easily as a huge specimen. This is a delicious stuffing mixture, which also works well with goose, duck, or chicken. The special ingredient is the candied fruits in a strong mustard syrup—otherwise known as Mostarda di Cremona. Far too good to save just for Christmas, which is not the tradition in Italy anyway—this is a fantastic choice for a Sunday roast lunch for eight people at any time of the year!

Serves 8

1 small turkey, weighing about 9lb
extra virgin olive oil, for basting
4 Italian sausages, skinned and crumbled
1 large apple, peeled and chopped
grated peel and juice of 1 lemon and 1 orange
2 stale white rolls, soaked in water to soften, then crumbled
1 large glass red wine
4oz pancetta, chopped fine
2 celery stalks, chopped fine
1 large onion, chopped fine
2 tablespoons Mostarda di Cremona, chopped
2 teaspoons finely chopped sage leaves
1 whole orange
sea salt and freshly ground black pepper

1 Preheat the oven to 375°F. Wipe the turkey carefully all over. Rub the bird with olive oil all over the outside and also on the inside.

2 Mix the sausages with the chopped apple, the citrus peel, the crumbled soaked rolls, red wine, pancetta, celery, onion, Mostarda, and sage very thoroughly and use this mixture to fill the turkey cavity at the neck end.

3 Place a whole orange in the other end. Sew the neck cavity closed with kitchen string. Place in a large roasting pan.

4 Season the bird thoroughly with salt and pepper, drizzle with more olive oil, and roast, breast-side down, in the oven for about 45 minutes. Baste, turn over, drizzle with olive oil again, and continue to roast, basting frequently for about 4 hours, or until the turkey is thoroughly cooked through.

5 Remove the turkey from the oven, allow to stand for about 10 minutes, then carve and serve. Delicious with Italian roast potatoes and braised artichokes.

VARIATION ~ Also delicious using goose instead of turkey. In either case use a free-range bird, which will give you lots of flavor and will taste genuinely rich and gutsy, like a proper farmyard animal! You could also use the stuffing (halving the quantity) to fill a chicken.

To eat an egg laid within the hour, bread made the same day, and drink wine from the new harvest can never do you harm.

Sicilian Proverb

quaglie in tegame

BRAISED QUAIL

These tender little birds cook quickly, so this is an extremely easy way to cook them to get the very best out of them, leaving them moist and succulent. If you are not that keen on polenta, serve with mashed potatoes and a green vegetable instead. The important thing is to enjoy all those delicious cooking juices, soaking them up with polenta, mashed potatoes, or some crusty bread.

Serves 4

**5 tablespoons olive oil
juice of 1 lemon
2 tablespoons chopped fresh Italian parsley
4 tablespoons Marsala
1 garlic clove, minced
8 oven-ready meaty quails
8 slices of pancetta
sea salt and freshly ground black pepper**

TO SERVE
grilled polenta

1 Preheat the oven to 425°F. Mix the olive oil, lemon juice, parsley, Marsala, garlic, and salt and pepper together in a large bowl. Place the quails in the mixture and let them stand for about 30 minutes, rubbing it all over the birds.

2 Wrap the marinated quails in the pancetta and put them in a large, ovenproof casserole dish.

3 Dilute the remaining marinade with a glass of water, stir and pour all over the birds. Cover the casserole and roast in the oven for about 20 minutes.

4 Serve the quails piping hot with slices of grilled polenta and their marinade juices poured over both quail and polenta.

I have never been particularly fond of the kind of tender, floppy fleshed chicken, which seems to require no chewing. Chickens at home in Italy were chewy, with a thin layer of fat between their skin and their rich pink flesh. They tasted completely different from most chickens I have eaten before or since. At home in Tuscany I learned how to wring a chicken's neck quickly and hopefully as painlessly as possible by the time I was about seven. It was never a task I relished, especially if the poor bird didn't die immediately or spent a long time twitching. The plucking and gutting process I always found completely riveting, probably this is where my early ambition to become a vet was born. The early ambition to become a vet was later superseded by a desire to go into the medical profession, but in the end my skills as a scientist were simply not up to the challenge. Our chickens were amazingly well fed. Not only did they enjoy their basic diet of corn and mash, but they also got to enjoy all our leftovers—when there were any!

Later, when I was married and living in England, I established another hen house and filled part of my garden with a flock of clucking, happy hens, with a strong rooster to keep them in line! I would use the bottom oven of my range to keep the baby chicks warm, and erected ever more complicated and heavy duty fencing to keep all foxes at bay. These chickens were kept mainly for their eggs, which tasted superb as a result of all my tender loving care and frequent leftover specials.

One of the greatest kitchen memories for me as a child was when a boiling fowl was kept simmering on the burner for hours, with carrots, onions, celery, and the odd tomato or cabbage leaf added to the water. When eventually the resulting stock was considered ready, the enormous, tough old chicken would be removed and placed to one side while the stock was carefully strained. The cooked chicken was wonderful to pick at for my brothers and I. We would eat the yellow yolks, now hard-cooked to a crumbly dustiness, which were to be found within the chicken. We would squabble loudly over who would get to eat the gizzard, boiled to a wonderfully chewy, dense consistency and so delicious when sliced and sprinkled with just a little salt. I have since tried to get my sons to react with the same level of enthusiasm, but sadly, though perhaps not surprisingly, they don't find the idea nearly as appealing as I did!

The only other birds I have had the occasion to try and keep have been guinea fowl, which turned out to be a lot less friendly than their chicken cousins. In the end I decided that although I liked to eat them, as far as keeping them is concerned, this is not the bird for me— too noisy, spiteful, and very unkind to my poor old hens. All 30 of them eventually ended up in the freezer!

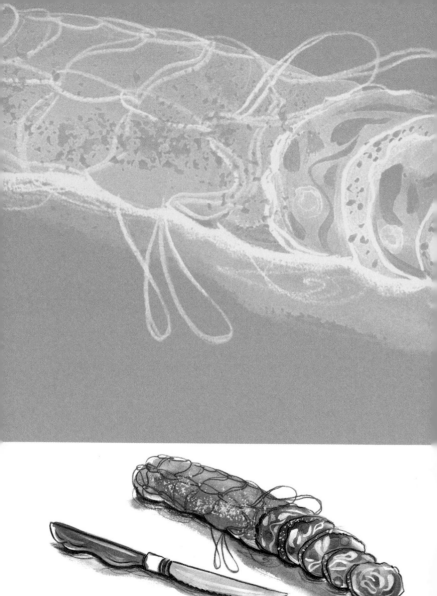

meat

saltimbocca alla romana

VEAL SCALLOPS WITH HAM, MOZZARELLA, AND SAGE

The name of this dish translates as 'jump into your mouth' indicating that it is so delicious that you can hardly keep it on the plate! It is a traditional Roman way of serving tender veal scallops, though for those of you who draw the line at eating veal, you could also use turkey or chicken breast. I have to say, however, that if you want to cook this dish in the classic style, then it really does have to be veal. Be careful not to use prosciutto that is too salty, so as not to overpower the other flavors in the dish. It is absolutely wonderful if cooked quickly and served as soon as it is ready.

∾

Serves 4

8 veal scallops
20 sage leaves
8 slices of fresh buffalo mozzarella
8 slices of prosciutto crudo
2 tablespoons butter
½ cup dry white wine
sea salt and freshly ground black pepper

1 Trim and batten the scallops so that they are all more or less the same size.

2 Place 2 sage leaves on each scallop, cover with a slice of mozzarella, then cover with a slice of prosciutto. If necessary, secure everything in place with a toothpick.

3 Melt the butter in a large skillet with a few sage leaves. Lay the scallops, prosciutto side down for about 2 or 3 minutes, then turn over very carefully and continue to cook on the other side for a further 2 or 3 minutes. Season to taste.

4 Remove the skillet from the heat. Take the cooked scallops out of the skillet and arrange in a large serving dish.

5 Return the skillet to the heat and add the wine. Boil quickly for 2 minutes, stirring to blend the juices with the wine to make a thin sauce.

6 Pour over the meat and serve immediately. If using toothpicks, remove them from the saltimbocca before serving.

scaloppine al marsala

VEAL SCALLOPS WITH MARSALA

Scaloppina is an integral part of every Italian kitchen. There are many versions—with wine, with herbs, with orange or lemon juice and peel, Vin Santo, Marsala, and others. Here is the classic Marsala version from Piemonte. The whole idea of cooking veal like this is that it must cook fast, so the process of battening the meat is very important to make sure that it is evenly flattened.

Serves 4

8 veal scallops
2 to 3 tablespoons all-purpose flour
2 tablespoons unsalted butter
½ cup Marsala
sea salt and freshly ground black pepper

1 Trim and batten the scallops carefully with a meat mallet until they are very thin, covering the meat with a sheet of plastic wrap to prevent it from tearing. Spread the flour out on a large plate, add the scallops, and toss lightly in the flour to coat, shaking off any excess.

2 Melt the butter in a large skillet. Add the scallops and quickly fry on both sides for 2 or 3 minutes. Season with salt and pepper.

3 Remove the meat from the skillet and arrange in a warmed serving dish. Pour the wine into the hot skillet.

4 Let the alcohol evaporate, then scrape the base of the skillet thoroughly to amalgamate the contents with the wine. Stir and reduce the sauce slightly before pouring over the meat. Serve immediately.

cotolette

BREADED VEAL SCALLOPS

This is a somewhat lighter version of the classic Milanese dish of the same name, which calls for a thick veal chop, coated in egg and bread crumbs, and fried in plenty of butter. The secret is to leave the scallops to soak thoroughly in the egg, so that the meat remains juicy and tender under the crisp breadcrumb coating.

∾

Serves 4

8 veal scallops
2 eggs
1½ cups very fine dry bread crumbs
sunflower oil, for pan-frying
sea salt and freshly ground black pepper

TO SERVE
lemon wedges

1 Trim and batten the scallops carefully with a meat mallet until very thin, covering the meat with a sheet of plastic wrap to prevent them from tearing.

2 Beat the eggs in a large, shallow bowl, then season with salt and pepper. Lay the meat in the beaten egg and allow to soak for about 1 hour.

3 Spread out the bread crumbs on a large plate. Drain each piece of meat and, using the heel of your hand, press the meat into the bread crumbs, shaking off any excess. Make sure the meat is completely coated.

4 Heat the sunflower oil in a large, wide skillet until sizzling hot. Add the scallops and quickly pan-fry for about 4 minutes on each side, or until crisp and golden brown.

5 Remove, drain, and lay on paper towels to absorb any excess oil. Serve with wedges of lemon.

This is Great w/ Cod !! :)

scaloppine al limone

VEAL SCALLOPS WITH LEMON

T he fresh quality of this recipe makes it a perfect dish for the summer. I like to serve it with steamed potatoes and a very crisp green salad, or some green beans dressed with a drizzle of olive oil. If veal is out of the question for you, use turkey or chicken breast instead.

∽

Serves 6

12 veal or 6 turkey scallops or small boneless chicken breasts
3 tablespoons all-purpose flour
2 tablespoons olive oil
2 tablespoons chopped fresh parsley
juice and grated peel of 1 lemon
2 tablespoons dry white wine
salt and freshly ground black pepper

TO SERVE
lemon wedges
sprigs of fresh herbs

1 Trim the meat, cut each piece in half and batten them all
evenly with a meat mallet, covering the meat with a sheet of
plastic wrap to prevent it from tearing. Spread the flour out on a
large plate, add the scallops, and toss lightly in the flour to coat,
shaking off any excess.

2 Heat the oil in a skillet. Add the meat and cook until sealed
on one side, turn it over and sprinkle with the parsley, lemon
peel, and juice. Reduce the heat and cook for an additional
4 minutes, then turn the meat over again.

3 Season with salt and pepper and cook until the meat is
cooked all the way through, about 5 minutes for thin turkey
or chicken, slightly less for veal.

4 Remove the meat from the skillet and arrange in a serving
dish. Pour the wine into the hot skillet, let the alcohol
evaporate, then scrape the base of the skillet thoroughly to
amalgamate the contents with the wine.

5 Tip the juices from the skillet over the meat, add the lemon
wedges and herbs, and serve immediately.

VARIATION ~ You can vary the flavor completely by using
orange juice and peel instead of lemon. Feel free to use some
other fresh herbs, apart from parsley, if you have them to hand.

bistecchine alla pizzaiola

BEEF PIZZAIOLA

The name of the dish indicates that it tastes like a basic pizza recipe, because it has the ingredients of pizza put together, only served with meat. The original topping for pizza was once just garlic, tomatoes, and oregano and, to confuse matters, it was called Marinara. The ratio of sauce to meat is completely unbalanced, so if you prefer, you could save some of the sauce to serve tossed through some freshly cooked pasta. It is essential that the meat hardly cooks at all, so it remains tender. There should be plenty of oregano and garlic to ensure that these flavors shine through the finished dish.

Serves 6

4 tablespoons olive oil
2 garlic cloves, chopped
1¼ cups puréed or canned chopped tomatoes
1 heaping teaspoon dried oregano
6 thinly cut beef minute steaks
sea salt and freshly ground black pepper

TO SERVE
crusty bread

1 Heat the olive oil in a wide skillet. Add the garlic and fry gently for about 5 minutes, then pour in the tomatoes.

2 Stir and leave to simmer for about 10 minutes, then add the oregano and season with salt and pepper to taste.

3 While the sauce simmers, trim off all fat and gristle from the steaks and batten them carefully with a meat mallet until thin, covering the meat with a sheet of plastic wrap to prevent it from tearing.

4 Place the steaks in the skillet, cover, and take off the heat. Leave to stand for 5 to 6 minutes so that the meat just cooks through.

5 Remove the steaks carefully from the skillet and arrange on a serving platter. Cover with the sauce and serve immediately with plenty of crusty bread to mop up all the sauce.

SERVING SUGGESTION ~ This recipe is also delicious served with a rich garlic mashed potato.

brasato al barolo

BRAISED BEEF IN BAROLO

This classic meat dish from Piemonte is often served with a steaming hot slab of polenta. It is very satisfying and filling and is also delicious made using venison instead of beef. You do need to make sure that a little bit of fat is left on the joint, and the extra richness and moisture is added by the pork fat inserted into the meat. You can use any other dense, strong red wine if Barolo is unavailable or just too expensive. I sometimes serve this with a selection of different purées: potato, celeriac, chestnut, and perhaps carrot for a splash of color.

When braising or stewing meat, make sure the heat is kept really low, so that the liquid around the meat barely moves during the cooking process. If you allow the pot to bubble audibly, the result will be a tough joint of meat at the end. It is much better to cook it slowly and for a longer period of time than to increase the heat.

Serves 6

about 3¼lb lean beef stewing joint
2oz pork fat, cut into thin strips
2 tablespoons chopped fresh parsley
1 teaspoon chopped fresh sage
½ tablespoon chopped fresh rosemary
2 garlic cloves, chopped fine
a pinch of nutmeg
a pinch of mixed spice
5 tablespoons all-purpose flour
5 tablespoons olive oil
1 tablespoon unsalted butter
1 onion, chopped
1 carrot, sliced
1 celery stalk, sliced
2 dried bay leaves
3 or 4 small fresh parsley sprigs
1 bottle Barolo, or other rich red wine
sea salt and freshly ground black pepper

1 Using a thick metal skewer, pierce the joint all over and insert the strips of pork fat wherever possible deep into the meat.

2 Mix the chopped parsley, sage, rosemary, and garlic together in a large bowl. Add plenty of salt and pepper, then mix in the spices and about half the flour.

3 Heat the olive oil and butter together in a large, heavy casserole dish for about 5 minutes. Add the onion and let it sizzle gently for a few minutes, stirring constantly.

4 Meanwhile, roll the joint in the herb mixture, then lay it gently on top of the onion in the casserole dish. Add the carrot, celery, bay leaves, and parsley sprigs.

5 Cook the meat, turning it over several times until sealed and browned, then remove it from the casserole dish and carefully drain off any excess fat from the casserole.

6 Add the remaining flour and mix it into the remaining cooked veg and all the cooking juices to make a smooth paste. Pour in about 2 glasses of red wine and stir together thoroughly. Allow the alcohol to evaporate for about 2 minutes, then return the meat to the casserole. Turn it over several times, then pour in the remaining wine and cover tightly.

7 Continue to simmer as gently as possible for about 4 hours, turning the joint occasionally. When the meat is completely tender, remove it from the casserole and push the sauce through a food mill.

8 Taste and adjust the seasoning if necessary. Slice the meat thickly onto a warm platter, cover with the sauce, and serve immediately.

The colder, rainier northern Italian regions are where cattle herds fare best, as the climate means that crops suitable for winter fodder are plentiful. This means that both Lombardy and Piemonte excel in recipes for both veal and beef. However, that is certainly not to say that other regions of Italy are also blessed with their very own beef and veal specialties. In particular the amazing Chianina cattle of Tuscany used to make the Florentine steak, and the delectable dish called Saltimbocca, from Rome, which consists of a thin slice of veal covered with mozzarella and ham, flavored with sage, and gently fried in butter and white wine.

Further south, beef and veal tend to practically disappear from the menu altogether, and are replaced by a little pork, some mutton or lamb, and a great deal of fish. There are of course some exceptions to this rule, in particular the famous Sicilian specialty of *Falsomagro*, which translates literally as "false lean." This is a wide sheet of beef skirt or steak, filled with everything from salami to hard cooked eggs, wrapped inside. This huge roll of stuffed beef is then stewed gently in a rich tomato sauce. The tendency to eat less red meat in the deep south of the coutnry is one of the reasons why the southern Italian diet is considered to be so very healthy.

ossobucco in umido

STEWED OSSOBUCCO

Ossobucco is the veal shank and can be bought prepared from your local butcher—always remember to ask for it to be cut from the hind shin of the veal where the meat is more tender. This version is the traditional way of serving ossobuco in a rich tomato-based sauce.

Serves 6

**3¼lb ossobucco steaks
4 celery stalks, chopped fine
1 large onion, chopped fine
2 carrots, chopped fine
3 garlic cloves, chopped fine
4 tablespoons olive oil
2 cups dry white wine
1 cup puréed tomatoes
2 tablespoons concentrated tomato paste, diluted in a
little warm water
sea salt and freshly ground black pepper**

1 Wipe the steaks to make sure there are no shards of bone. Place all the vegetables and oil into a heavy casserole dish large enough to take all the meat as well.

2 Fry the vegetables and the oil together for about 10 minutes or until softened. Remove the vegetables with a slotted spoon, and reserve until required.

3 Add the meat to the casserole dish and brown carefully on both sides. Add half the wine and boil quickly for 1 minute, then reduce the heat and add the tomatoes and tomato paste. Season with salt and pepper, then cover and simmer, stirring frequently and basting with the remaining wine, for about 2 hours, or until very tender.

NOTE ~ Served traditionally with a plain white or a saffron risotto or with mashed potato and gremolata, which is a mixture of chopped fresh Italian parsley and grated lemon peel.

involtini

STUFFED BEEF OLIVES

I find this dish immensely comforting and if the beef used is tasty, it can be a really memorable dish. This is another one of those dishes that has a thousand different versions of the same basic recipe and which also tastes better eaten a day later, when the meat has had a chance to absorb the flavours of all the other ingredients. It is also good made with thin pork steaks.

Serves 6

**about 2¼lb skirt steak, sliced into 12 little slices
weighing about 3oz each
6oz prosciutto crudo, roughly chopped
2 garlic cloves, chopped
3 carrots, cut into 12 batons
3 celery stalks, cut into 12 batons
3 tablespoons olive oil
1 onion, finely chopped
1lb fresh ripe tomatoes, peeled, seeded, and roughly chopped
or 1¾ cups canned chopped tomatoes
sea salt and freshly ground black pepper**

TO SERVE
mashed potatoes or freshly cooked rice

1 Trim the meat neatly, putting any scraps to one side to use in another recipe. Batten the meat with a meat mallet until the slices are of even thickness, covering them with a sheet of plastic wrap to prevent it from tearing.

2 Place a little chopped prosciutto, a little chopped garlic, and a baton each of carrot and celery in the center of each slice of meat.

3 Roll up the slice of meat around the filling and secure with toothpicks.

4 Heat the olive oil in a wide skillet. Add the onion and cook for a few minutes or until the onion is soft, then add the tomatoes. Season to taste, cover, and simmer for about 5 minutes. Arrange the beef olives in the skillet, cover, and cook for an additional 50 minutes, turning over the beef olives frequently.

5 Arrange the cooked beef olives on a bed of mashed potatoes or rice, remove the toothpicks, drizzle over all the remaining sauce, and serve.

bistecca alla fiorentina

FLORENTINE T-BONE STEAK

The whole point about this steak is that it is enormous—made in Tuscany from the very best Chianina cattle. If you adopt the same marinade and cooking methods for a tenderloin or porterhouse steak or a thick sirloin, you will have some of the flavor, but not the overwhelming size factor, which is part of the whole experience!

Serves 2

8 tablespoons olive oil
4 or 5 fresh rosemary sprigs
3 garlic cloves, crushed
1 bone-in T-bone steak weighing about 1¾ pounds
sea salt and freshly ground black pepper

1 Mix the olive oil, rosemary, garlic, salt and pepper together in a large, shallow dish. Add the steak and leave to marinate for 24 to 48 hours.

2 Preheat a broiler or light a barbecue. Broil to your personal preference under a broiler or on a barbecue.

3 When cooked to your taste, drizzle with a little of the best extra virgin olive oil, season with salt and pepper to taste, and serve.

NOTE ~ For anybody who has ever eaten a Fiorentina in Tuscany, this will only just hint at the real thing!

spezzatino di manzo

BEEF STEW

Make sure the meat has sufficient time to cook so that it becomes really tender—you should be able to almost cut through it with a spoon. As with all slow-cooked stews ensure that the meat is of the best possible quality and full of flavor. Keep the heat so low that the liquid around the meat barely moves. If you don't want to use beef, try lamb or pork instead, or even game, such as wild boar or venison.

Serves 6

about 3¼lb stewing or braising beef
5 tablespoons olive oil
2 or 3 fresh sage leaves
2 or 3 fresh rosemary sprigs
4 tablespoons tomato paste, diluted in ½ cup warm water
1¾ cups canned chopped tomatoes, drained
beef broth for basting
1lb potatoes, peeled and cubed
3 cups shelled fresh or frozen peas
4 large carrots, cubed
sea salt and freshly ground black pepper

TO SERVE
puréed potatoes, rice, or polenta

1 Trim the meat and cut it into even-size cubes. Heat the olive oil in a casserole dish with the herbs for a few minutes, then add the meat and cook until sealed and browned all over.

2 When the meat is well browned, reduce the heat and pour in the diluted tomato paste and the chopped tomatoes.

3 Pour in enough broth to just cover the meat, cover, and allow to simmer very gently for about 30 to 45 minutes. Stir occasionally.

4 Add the potatoes, peas, and carrots. Cover and continue to cook for a further 20 to 30 minutes, or until the vegetables are cooked.

5 Taste and adjust seasoning as required, then transfer to a platter and serve immediately with puréed potatoes or rice or polenta.

abbacchio alla romana

ROMAN ROAST LAMB

A delicious way of serving young lamb. The surprise ingredients are the salty anchovies and the sour bite of the vinegar, which cuts the sweetness of the lamb to perfection. This is a Roman specialty in springtime, when young lamb is traditionally plentiful.

∽

Serves 4

2¼lb very young, tender lamb on the bone, cut into chunks the size of a small apple
3 tablespoons olive oil
knob of butter
1 lamb's kidney, cubed
1 cup dry white wine or water
2 fresh rosemary sprigs
2 large anchovies preserved in salt, or 5 canned anchovy fillets in oil, drained well
4 garlic cloves, peeled
4 to 5 tablespoons red wine vinegar
salt and freshly ground black pepper

1 Wipe the meat carefully all over in case of bone shards. Set a wide, deep skillet with a heavy base over a low heat. Pour in the olive oil, add the butter, and heat together for 5 minutes.

2 Add the kidney and meat chunks to the hot fat and cook until sealed and browned. Season generously with salt and pepper and reduce the heat.

3 Cover and allow to simmer gently for 45 minutes, basting occasionally with a little wine or water and turning the meat occasionally.

4 Meanwhile, place the leaves from the rosemary, the anchovies, and garlic in a mortar, and using a pestle, pound briefly.

5 Stir in the vinegar and pour this mixture over the meat. Stir thoroughly, and simmer for a further 5 minutes until the acidic fumes of the vinegar have evaporated before serving.

il polpettone

ITALIAN MEATLOAF

This is a meatloaf, stewed in tomato sauce and usually served warm. Especially popular in Naples, it uses the same kind of mixture as used for Polpette (see page 260).

Serves 6 to 8

1¼lb fresh ground veal, beef, or pork
2 cups soft, fine white bread crumbs
1⅓ cups Parmigiano Reggiano, freshly grated
2 large eggs, beaten
6 tablespoons chopped fresh Italian parsley
1 large onion, chopped fine
½ teaspoon grated lemon peel
¼ teaspoon freshly grated nutmeg
¼ cup cold water
8 tablespoons fine dry white bread crumbs
6 tablespoons olive oil
1 large onion, sliced thin
2 cups puréed or canned chopped tomatoes
sea salt and freshly ground black pepper

1 Place the ground meat, soft white bread crumbs, cheese, beaten eggs, parsley, finely chopped onion, lemon peel, nutmeg, and water in a large bowl and mix together.

2 Season with salt and pepper, and shape into a loaf. Spread out the fine, dry bread crumbs on a large plate, add the meatloaf and roll it in the bread crumbs.

3 Heat the olive oil in a large skillet. Add half the sliced onion and fry gently until soft. Lay the loaf on top, then turn it over to seal and brown it thoroughly. Add the remaining sliced onion and fry for a further 5 minutes, before adding the tomatoes.

4 Cover and cook slowly for 2 hours, turning frequently. Serve thickly sliced with the sauce. Alternatively, use the sauce to dress freshly cooked pasta.

polpette al pomodoro

MEATBALLS IN TOMATO SAUCE

There must be a thousand ways to make polpette, *Italian meatballs, but the recipe I have given here is more or less the best-loved one in Italy. In lean times, when meat was scarce, the quantity of bread would be increased—it remains a good way of making the recipe stretch! The meatballs are fried first, before being immersed into the sauce, so that they do not disintegrate and make a rather strange and lumpy Bolognese type sauce!*

Serves 4

14oz fresh ground veal, beef, turkey, chicken, or pork
2 cups soft, fine white bread crumbs
1⅓ cups freshly grated, Parmigiano Reggiano
1 large egg, beaten
4 tablespoons chopped fresh Italian parsley
½ teaspoon grated lemon peel
¼ teaspoon freshly grated nutmeg
¼ cup cold water
6 tablespoons fine dry white bread crumbs
6 tablespoons olive oil
sea salt and freshly ground black pepper

SAUCE
3 tablespoons olive oil
2 garlic cloves, thinly sliced or crushed into a purée
1¾ puréed or canned tomatoes
about 9 leaves fresh basil, torn into small sections
with your fingers
sea salt and freshly ground black pepper

TO SERVE
mashed potatoes or rice

1 Place the meat, soft bread crumbs, cheese, egg, salt, pepper,
parsley, lemon peel, and nutmeg in a large bowl and mix
thoroughly, then gradually blend in the water. Mix with your
hands for a few minutes, then shape the mixture into small balls
about the size of a golf ball. Spread out the dry white bread crumbs
on a plate, add the meatballs and coat with the bread crumbs.

2 Heat about 6 tablespoons of olive oil in a large skillet. Add the meatballs and fry for 5 to 6 minutes or until cooked through and crisp on the outside. Drain on paper towels.

3 Meanwhile, make the sauce. Heat the olive oil in a heavy pan or skillet. Add the garlic and fry gently until soft. Pour in the tomatoes and stir carefully.

4 Cover and allow to simmer for about 20 minutes, or until the sauce is glossy and thick. Add the basil and stir. Season to taste and cover.

5 Simmer for an additional 5 minutes, then place all the meatballs in the pan. Make sure the meatballs are well covered in the sauce and allow to simmer for a further 10 minutes. Serve hot with mashed potatoes or rice.

SERVING SUGGESTION ~ You can also serve these meatballs covered in the sauce and cold as part of a buffet or picnic; though in this case I would suggest you make them slightly smaller. Of course you don't need to cover them with the sauce, just serve them crisp and freshly fried at the end of step 2.

maiale al latte

PORK BRAISED IN MILK

This dish originally comes from the Trieste area in Friuli, in northeastern Italy. I find it always tastes better the day after I've made it. By the time the pork has been marinated and then slowly stewed in milk, the final texture should be like stewed fruit, soft and juicy enough to slice through with a spoon. It is worth using free-range, best quality pork as you will end up with a much thicker sauce—cheap meat tends to release a lot of water during cooking. I always think that it is not the more expensive cut of meat which will make the difference, just better quality meat to start with! I prefer to make it with a leg of pork, which is tasty, and I serve with it a thin prune and apple sauce, flavored with grated lemon and orange peel.

Serves 6

5½lb pork loin, all skin and fat removed
½ cup olive oil
4 large garlic cloves, sliced thin
a handful of fresh sage leaves
4 cups whole milk
thinly grated peel of 2 lemons
juice of 1 lemon
sea salt and freshly ground black pepper

1 Preheat the oven to 400°F. Wipe and trim the pork as necessary. Heat the olive oil in an ovenproof casserole dish until sizzling. The dish must be large enough to hold the meat and milk comfortably, while allowing the meat to remain mostly submerged in the milk.

2 Add the pork loin to the casserole and cook until browned all over. Remove the meat and drain off the excess fat.

3 Remove the casserole dish from the heat. Add the garlic and sage to the casserole, then return the browned meat to the casserole, bone side down. Season with salt and pepper and pour over the milk.

4 Return the casserole dish to the heat and bring to a boil, then remove from the heat and add the lemon peel and juice. Allow the milk to curdle slightly, then cover with a lid and roast in the oven for 20 minutes.

5 Reduce the heat to 300°F and continue to cook, covered, for an additional 90 minutes, adding more milk as necessary and basting and turning the loin joint.

6 Remove the casserole from the oven. Allow the meat to rest for 5 minutes, then carve and serve with the milky juices from the dish.

NOTE ~ It is often the cheaper cuts of meat that have the most flavor, though they may not look as tidy or carve as neatly as the more expensive cuts. In the case of pork, the leg or shoulder will both work very well in this recipe, giving a deliciously tasty result, although it may look slightly scruffier than the loin. Whichever cut you choose, please make sure that the pork is free range if possible and of good quality. You can also cook a joint of boneless veal in exactly the same way.

arista di maiale alla fiorentina

ROASTED LOIN OF PORK IN THE FLORENTINE TRADITION

According to Tuscan kitchen lore, this dish has Renaissance origins. They say it was especially created for the Ecumenical Council in Florence, the year that the Greek Orthodox Church was invited for the first time. In those days of very slow and perilous travel, nobody was quite sure how long it might take the esteemed guests to arrive. So they had to create a dish which would "hold" over several days before becoming completely rotten and inedible. The natural preservative qualities of rosemary, pepper, and garlic, mixed with plenty of salt, would not only have helped to keep the meat fresh, but would have masked any unpleasant odor! When the Greeks arrived, they pronounced the dish Aristos, which means excellent in ancient Greek, and so the name of the dish has stuck through history.

It is the kind of roast that works best with larger joints of meat rather than smaller ones, as with smaller joints the meat tends to dry out. The bigger the piece of meat, the more moist and juicy it will be at the end.

Serves 6

3 tablespoons fresh rosemary leaves, washed
8 large garlic cloves, puréed
4 or 5 tablespoons olive oil
3¼–4½lb pork loin, boned, fat and skin removed
¾ cup dry white wine
sea salt and freshly ground black pepper

1 Preheat the oven to 350°F. Using a sharp knife finely chop the rosemary and mix it into the puréed garlic. Season with salt and plenty of pepper. Add enough olive oil to make a thick paste.

2 Using a skewer or long sharp knife, make lots of deep incisions in the meat. Insert the rosemary paste into the meat, pushing it deep inside the flesh with your fingers.

3 Tie the joint securely with kitchen string and rub it all over with olive oil. Season the exterior with salt and pepper. Place the joint in a large roasting pan.

4 Roast in the oven for about 2 hours, basting frequently with the juices from the pan and the white wine. Turn it over each time you baste. Either let the pork cool and serve cold, or eat piping hot.

rognoni al vino bianco

KIDNEYS WITH WHITE WINE

Kidneys are the most popular and widely used variety meat in Italian cooking after liver. I prefer to use veal kidneys when I can find them, and always from very young animals, so they are tender and sweet tasting. It is vital to cook kidneys as briefly as possible to prevent them from becoming hard and chewy. Allow time for the kidneys to soak in the milk for an hour or so before cooking so that all the impurities can be drawn out.

Serves 4

3 cups milk
**2¼lb kidneys, preferably veal, cleaned carefully and cut
into small cubes**
3 tablespoons all-purpose flour
4 tablespoons olive oil
3 garlic cloves, sliced fine
2 tablespoons chopped fresh Italian parsley
½ cup dry white wine
sea salt and freshly ground black pepper

1 Pour the milk into a large bowl, add the kidneys, and allow to soak for 1 hour, then drain and wash very thoroughly under cold running water. Dry on paper towels. Spread out the flour on a plate, add the kidneys, and toss lightly in the flour. Shake off any excess flour.

2 Heat the olive oil in a skillet. Add the garlic and fry gently until the garlic is just browned.

3 Add the kidneys and fry quickly until browned all over, then add the parsley and wine.

4 Cook for an additional 3 minutes, then season with salt and pepper to taste and serve immediately.

NOTE ~ The white membrane should be removed from all kidneys before cooking. Snip the membrane and fat where it is connected to the core and peel it away with your fingers.

fegato alla veneziana

LIVER IN THE VENETIAN STYLE

The secret here is to make sure the liver is barely cooked, it must not be allowed to become leathery and tough. Plenty of sweet red onions and a pile of creamy mashed potato make this a real treat.

Serves 4

1¼lb calf's liver, cut into very thin slices
2¼lb red onions
3 tablespoons vegetable oil
1 tablespoon unsalted butter
a handful of fresh parsley, chopped fine
½ cup dry white wine
sea salt and freshly ground black pepper

1 Trim the liver carefully, pulling off the transparent, rind-like skin from around each slice and removing any gristle.

2 Using a sharp knife, slice the onions evenly and very thinly. Rinse the onions under cold running water, then drain and pat dry with paper towels.

3 Heat the vegetable oil and butter in a large skillet. Add the onions and parsley and fry slowly over a very low heat for 1 hour, covered, until shiny and soft. Stir frequently to avoid sticking or burning.

4 Increase the heat, move the onions to one side and lay the liver in the skillet. Fry quickly until browned on both sides. Pour the wine over it as it browns, the liver will cook in about 3 minutes. Season with salt and pepper to taste.

5 Remove the liver from the skillet and keep it warm. Arrange the cooked onions on a warmed serving platter, lay the liver on top and serve immediately, surrounded by mashed potato.

The second course, *il secondo*, which in traditional Italian cooking and eating habits follows a pasta, soup, or risotto course *(il primo)*, is generally not as important as the first course. In fact, in many modern Italian households, families quite regularly choose to eat either a main course or a first course, but often not both. The main course can be meat, fish, vegetable, egg, or cheese, or a combination of several of these.

The golden age of four-course lunches followed by four hour siestas is not quite as popular as it used to be, except on special occasions like weddings, birthdays, and so on. In these meals, pasta and/or risotto, a main course of meat or fish, and finally dessert or fruit or both follows antipasti.

In Italian homes, the meat that is cooked on a daily basis tends to be very lean, as nowadays this is what the average housewife likes to feed to her family. Meat is usually cooked in the simplest possible way, allowing the taste of the meat itself to shine. Very, very rarely are complex sauces permitted to cloud the existing flavor of good quality meat. The "contorno" or accompanying vegetables are also extremely important, although they are usually very simply presented.

If I had to identify which region of Italy features meat most strongly in its repertoire of dishes, I would have to say it is actually not a region but the city of Rome. The central abattoir of the city, called *il Testaccio* (no longer a slaughterhouse but a fashionable venue for Roman nightlife), is surrounded by several restaurants which still uphold the old traditions of Roman meat cooking. These recipes, some of which can immediately be identified as being not for the faint hearted, have their origins in a time when the meat prepared inside *il Testaccio* was destined for the upper classes of Rome, but the work done inside the building was done by people from the very lower levels of Roman society. At the end of each work shift, these workers would be allowed to gather up whatever scraps were left on the floor and take them home. Interestingly, it is these dishes, created with the very cheapest cuts of meat and variety meats that have become classical Italian recipes. As refrigeration had not been invented and Rome was often incredibly hot, some of this meat would have definitely been past its sell-by date. To cover up the flavor and smell emanating from these scraps, very strong smelling tastes were combined with the meat to make it palatable. Hence many of these recipes contain spices like cloves, dried chile, and huge amounts of garlic, along with sweet smelling herbs like mint and sage.

The selection of various different kinds of meat dishes in this chapter represent some of the most popular and traditional recipes cooked in Italian households all over the country.

desserts

crostata di frutta

FRUIT TART

When I was growing up in Tuscany, there was just one shop which made and sold the very best fruit tarts I have ever tasted. Bicycling home the four miles, balancing anything up to three of these on the handle bars and getting them home intact was an act in itself! This recipe is an attempt to re-create the flavor of those memories.

Makes one 9in tart

3 cups all-purpose flour, plus extra for dusting
¾ cup superfine sugar
a pinch of salt
2 eggs
grated peel of 1 unwaxed lemon
⅔ cup unsalted butter, softened, plus extra for greasing
8oz lightly poached apples, pears, apricots, or peaches
(if the stone fruit is really ripe and soft, don't poach,
but use it as it is)
1 egg yolk, beaten
confectioners' sugar, for dusting

1 Mix the flour with one third of the superfine sugar, salt, and lemon peel. Pile the flour mixture onto a countertop and make a hollow in the center with your fist.

2 Break two eggs into the hollow and add the butter and remaining sugar. Knead all this together quickly to form a smooth ball of dough. Wrap it in plastic wrap or a clean cloth and rest in a cool place, but not the refrigerator, for about 20 minutes.

3 Preheat the oven to 375°F. Divide the dough into 2 sections, one larger than the other. Roll out the larger piece evenly on a lightly floured countertop.

4 Grease and lightly flour the tart pan. Line the tart pan with the rolled out pastry and fill with the cooked fruit.

5 Roll out the smaller piece of dough and cut into strips. Arrange the strips as a lattice over the fruit. Brush lightly with the egg yolk and bake in the oven for about 35 minutes, or until golden brown, Leave to cool, dust lightly with confectioners' sugar and serve.

NOTE ~ When using soft berries, the pastry is rolled out to a wider disk and used to line a 10in tart pan, then lined with baking parchment and baking beans to bake blind until crisp in a preheated oven at 375°F (but watch carefully in case it burns). When completely cold, it is covered with a thin layer of cold, sweet custard and covered with raspberries, strawberries, or other soft fruit. A dusting of confectioners' sugar finishes off this delicious tart.

crostata di marmellata

ITALIAN JAM TART

This jam tart is made as a teatime treat for children all over the country. The pastry tends to be traditionally sweet, but you can reduce the amount of sugar if you prefer. At home in Tuscany, surfaces such as the kitchen tables, windowsills, or shelves were made of beautiful, cool marble, perfect for cooling a tart as quickly as possible! My favorite preserve for crostata is still plum, peach, or apricot, as the taste is inextricably linked to my happy childhood teas.

Makes one 9in tart

3 cups all-purpose flour, plus extra for dusting
¾ cup superfine sugar
a pinch of salt
grated peel of 1 unwaxed lemon
2 eggs
⅔ cup unsalted butter, softened, plus extra for greasing
1 jar of preserve of your choice
1 egg, beaten

1 Mix the flour with one third of the sugar, salt, and lemon peel. Pile the flour mixture onto a countertop and make a hollow in the center with your fist.

2 Break 2 eggs into the hollow and add the butter and remaining sugar. Knead all this together quickly to form a smooth ball of dough. Wrap it in plastic wrap or a clean cloth and rest in a cool place, but not the refrigerator, for about 20 minutes.

3 Preheat the oven to 400°F. Divide the dough into 2 sections, one larger than the other. Roll out the larger piece evenly on a lightly floured countertop.

4 Grease and lightly flour the tart pan. Line the tart pan with the rolled out pastry and fill with the preserve. Smooth the preserve over the pastry evenly.

5 Roll out the second piece of pastry and cut into strips. Arrange the strips of pastry over the preserve as a lattice and brush with the beaten egg.

6 Bake in the oven for about 30 minutes, or until golden brown and the pastry is crisp. Allow to cool completely before serving.

gelato alla crema

VANILLA ICE CREAM

*I*ce cream is as synonymous with Italian food as pasta, pizza, or cannelloni—perhaps even more so! Originally invented as a form of sorbet in Sicily during the Arab domination hundreds of years ago, using Etna's snow mixed with wine, honey, or fruit juice, ice cream has evolved in a variety of ways. Strange to say, the simplest recipe and the one that must be closest to the original ancient Arabic version, granita di limone, is still so very popular. Here is the basic recipe for simple Italian vanilla ice cream which all kinds of other ingredients can be added to create different flavors. Best results are to be had with a churning ice cream machine.

∽

Serves 6

5 egg yolks
¾ cup superfine sugar
2 cups whole milk
1 tablespoon vanilla extract

1 Beat the egg yolks and the sugar together until light, fluffy, and foaming. Place the milk in a pan and bring to just under a boil, do not allow it to boil.

2 Gradually strain the milk into the egg yolks, beating constantly. Never add more milk until the previous amount has been absorbed into the egg yolks and sugar. Return to the heat and reheat, stirring constantly, never allowing the mixture to boil.

3 When it is thickened enough to coat the back of a spoon, stir in the vanilla extract and remove from the heat. Strain and allow to cool completely.

4 Pour into an ice cream machine and churn until frozen and thickened to the right texture. Depending upon the machine, this will take either about 30 minutes or up to 1½ hours.

5 Alternatively, if you do not have an ice cream machine, pour the mixture into a freezerproof container and place in the freezer. You must then regularly stir the mixture from time to time to prevent ice crystals from forming.

panna cotta

This delicious Piedmontese specialty is gaining in popularity and fame all over Italy and beyond. You can make it completely plain or add crushed amaretti, coffee, chocolate, soft fruits, lemon or orange peel, liqueur—the possibilities are endless. The skill of this dessert lies in getting it to set without making it rubbery, so just the right amount of sheet gelatin needs to be used. Here is the basic, plain version.

Serves 8

3 to 4 sheets gelatin (colla di pesce)
4 cups light cream
8 tablespoons confectioners' sugar

FLAVORING
grated peel of l lemon, 1 small cup of espresso coffee,
3 tablespoons liqueur or brandy, or 2 teaspoons vanilla extract

CARAMEL
4 tablespoons superfine sugar

TO DECORATE
instant coffee powder
grated lemon peel
fruit coulis

1 Soak the sheets of gelatin in enough water to cover and leave
until spongy. Remove from the water and squeeze dry gently.

2 Divide the cream into two halves and bring to just under a
boil in two separate pans. Add the confectioners' sugar to
one half of the cream and add the soaked gelatin to the other.

3 Beat both halves constantly, one after the other, until the
sugar and gelatin have completely dissolved and the cream is
very hot but NOT boiling.

4 Pour both halves into one bowl and beat together. Add the flavoring of your choice and stir. Allow to cool completely.

5 While the mixture is cooling, coat the base of 8 ramekin molds with the superfine sugar and melt the sugar over a low flame to caramelize.

6 Alternatively, caramelize the sugar in a small pan and then pour it into the molds. Make sure the caramel is only just colored, so that it will not color the set panna cotta at all. Allow to cool.

7 Strain the panna cotta into the molds and leave to set in the refrigerator until required.

8 When firmly set dip the molds into boiling water for 5 seconds and turn out onto cold plates.

9 Decorate with a sprinkling of coffee, a grating of lemon peel, a fruit coulis, or whatever you feel is appropriate.

SERVING SUGGESTION ~ If you do not feel confident enough to turn the panna cotta out onto plates, serve it in small ramekins or cups instead. You can make a coffee version and froth the cream before setting to look like a cappuccino, served in a coffee cup set on a saucer.

> *I've learned here that simplicity is liberating. We no longer measure, but just cook. As all cooks know, ingredients of the moment are the best guides. Much of what we do is too simple to be called a recipe – it's just the way we do it.*

Frances Mayes, *Under the Tuscan Sun*

pere cotte nel vino rosso

PEARS POACHED IN RED WINE

Choose pears that are firm enough to poach and remain whole and intact during the cooking process. Also make sure they are all the same size so they cook simultaneously! The longer you leave the cooked pears in the wine the darker and more intensely flavored they become.

Serves 6

6 firm pears, peeled, left whole with stalks on
½ cinnamon stick
5 tablespoons superfine sugar
1 bottle good red wine

TO SERVE
cream, ice cream, or mascarpone cheese

1 Place the pears upright in a large, wide saucepan, slicing off the bottom of each pear in order to make it stand upright.

2 Add the cinnamon and sugar. Pour over the wine and bring to a boil, then reduce the heat to minimum.

3 Cover and simmer very slowly until the pears are soft, frequently turning them in the wine as they cook so that they become completely soaked and colored by the wine.

4 Transfer the pears to a bowl and allow to cool, turning frequently. Remove the cinnamon stick.

5 Serve the pears on their own or with cream, ice cream, or plain mascarpone. You may like to reduce the wine to a syrup, having drained the pears, and then drizzle the syrup over the fruit.

pesche al forno

BAKED PEACHES

If peaches are not available, this recipe works equally well with nectarines or very large plums. The firmer the fruit, the easier it will be to pit and fill, although the fruit may taste slightly sour. At the very end of the peach season, when they tend to be very woolly they are best used for cooking in a recipe such as this or in a tart.

❧

Serves 6

6 large peaches of the variety which will split in half quite easily
6 amaretti cookies, crumbled fine
1 tablespoon unsalted butter, plus extra for greasing
¼ cup granulated sugar
3 talespoons chopped, blanched almonds
⅔ cup dessert wine

1 Preheat the oven to 375°F. Cut the peaches in half. Remove the pit and scoop out about half of the flesh.

2 Mash the removed flesh with the crumbled amaretti cookies, the butter, sugar, and almonds. Dampen this mixture with a little wine, just enough to make a sticky texture. Fill all the peaches evenly with the mixture.

3 Arrange the peaches in a greased ovenproof dish and surround with the remaining wine.

4 Cover loosely with foil and bake in the oven for about 30 minutes, basting occasionally, until the peaches are tender.

5 Remove the foil and increase the heat of the oven for a few minutes to turn the tops of the peaches slightly crisp. Alternatively, place under a hot broiler for about 5 minutes. Serve hot or cold.

SERVING SUGGESTION ~ Delicious with mascarpone cheese, cream, zabaglione, or ice cream, although my favorite accompaniment is a scoop of peach sorbet.

semifreddo al cioccolato

ITALIAN CHOCOLATE ICE CREAM PARFAIT

This very easy dessert has a name which means almost cold or frozen, indicating a different texture to the smooth creaminess of the classic gelato. Semifreddo comes in many versions and almost always contains some form of alcohol to ensure that the mixture retains a certain softness. When removed from the freezer, it may be rather hard, so allow it to stand for a little while until it slices easily.

Serves 6

1 cup milk
6oz best quality baking chocolate
¾ cup superfine sugar
2½ cups heavy cream
3 tablespoons confectioners' sugar, sifted
1 tablespoon vanilla extract
2 tablespoons brandy
2 handfuls of crushed meringues

TO SERVE
melted bittersweet chocolate

1 Measure out ⅔ cup of the milk and finely chop the chocolate. Place the milk in a saucepan, stir the chocolate into the milk and melt it very slowly over a very low heat. Stir constantly until smooth. Remove the pan from the heat.

2 Place the remaining milk in a second saucepan with the superfine sugar. Heat until the sugar has dissolved but without boiling.

3 Pour the hot sweet milk into the chocolate mixture and beat together thoroughly until smooth. Continue to beat until cooled completely.

4 Place the cream in a large bowl and whip until stiff, then beat the confectioners' sugar through it. Stir the vanilla extract into the cream, then fold the cream into the cooled chocolate mixture. Add the brandy and crushed meringues.

5 Turn the mixture into a loaf or ring mold and freeze for about 4 hours, bearing in mind that the brandy will prevent the dessert from freezing completely.

6 Remove from the freezer, slice into wedges, and serve in a pool of bittersweet chocolate.

spumone di fragole

ITALIAN STRAWBERRY PARFAIT

A real childhood favorite for me. My original recipe is written in pencil in my dear mother's handwriting on an old yellowed piece of card. I remember she always made it in a loaf pan.

Serves 6

3¼ cups fresh strawberries, hulled
2 tablespoons strawberry liqueur or very sweet balsamic vinegar
5 tablespoons mascarpone or ricotta cheese
juice of ½ lemon
2 cups heavy cream, whipped and sweetened
with 3 tablespoons confectioners' sugar
1½ cups confectioners' sugar
12 large fresh strawberries, sliced,
or 2 handfuls of wild strawberries, left whole

TO SERVE
fresh strawberries
fresh mint leaves
strawberry liqueur or sweet, thick balsamic vinegar

1 Purée the whole strawberries by pushing them through a strainer into a bowl. Add the liqueur or vinegar.

2 Stir in the mascarpone or ricotta, then add the lemon juice and mix. Fold the sweetened cream into this mixture, then gently sift in the confectioners' sugar, folding it in very gradually and carefully.

3 Finally, fold the sliced or wild strawberries through the mixture. Pour into a freezerproof container with a lid and freeze for about 2 hours, giving it a stir twice or three times during freezing to prevent any ice crystals from forming. Don't worry if you end up with a few small crystals, the slightly gritty texture of this dessert is correct and typical.

SERVING SUGGESTION ~ Dip the mold into boiling hot water for 10 seconds, then turn out onto a platter and slice into six portions. Place each slice on a plate with a few strawberries, a few mint leaves, and a drizzle of strawberry liqueur or sweet balsamic vinegar. If you can leave the dessert to stand for up to 15 minutes before serving, so much the better.

NOTE ~ To make balsamic vinegar sweet and thick, boil quickly in a pan until reduced to a syrup texture. Allow to cool and use as required.

tiramisu classico al caffé

CLASSIC TIRAMISU WITH COFFEE

A classic Italian dessert originally created by a Mama to make her boy feel better after an illness—the idea being that the egg is nourishing and that by combining with sugar and mascarpone, then flavoring it with coffee and chocolate, you end up with something appealing to a recovering appetite! Here is the most basic, classic recipe, which can be elaborated on according to your imagination.

Serves 6

2 cups mascarpone or very rich cream cheese
4 eggs, separated
4 tablespoons superfine sugar
2 teaspoons espresso coffee
8 tablespoons weak coffee
6 tablespoons rum, Marsala, or brandy
about 20 ladyfingers
2 teaspoons cocoa powder
2 teaspoons finely ground coffee

1 Place the cheese in a large bowl and beat until soft and manageable. Beat the egg yolks in a separate bowl, until pale, then beat them into the cheese. Very gradually add the sugar to the cheese mixture, stirring and beating constantly. Pour in the espresso coffee and mix thoroughly.

2 Beat the egg whites in a clean, greasefree bowl until very stiff, then fold them into the egg mixture. Mix the weak coffee and the alcohol together in a small bowl.

3 Dip half the ladyfingers into the coffee mixture one at a time and use to line the base of a bowl. Pour in half the cheese mixture.

4 Dip the remaining ladyfingers in the liquid and arrange over the creamy layer. Pour over the remaining creamy mixture.

5 Bang the dish down lightly to settle the layers. Mix the cocoa and ground coffee together and sift over the dessert. Leave to chill for at least 3 hours, preferably overnight before serving.

torta al cioccolato

ITALIAN CHOCOLATE CAKE

*C*hocolate cake remains a great favorite with children and adults alike. This is a fairly foolproof cake that comes out light and moist every time. Please make sure that you use very good-quality chocolate with a very high cocoa content for the best possible results.

∽

Serves 6-8

8oz chocolate
⅔ cup unsalted butter, cubed
1 espresso coffee, about 2 tablespoons very strong black coffee
5 large eggs, separated
1 cup superfine sugar
1 teaspoon baking powder
2 tablespoons cocoa powder
1 cup all-purpose flour
confectioners' sugar, for dusting

1 Preheat the oven to 350°F. Line and grease a 9in loose-based cake pan.

2 Chop the chocolate, place in a large, heatproof bowl set over a pan of simmering water and melt gently. When the chocolate has melted, stir in the butter, then add the coffee.

3 Meanwhile, beat the egg whites in a clean, greasefree bowl until stiff, then gradually fold in the sugar. Mix the baking powder, cocoa powder, and flour together in a separate bowl.

4 Remove the chocolate from the heat, stir in the egg yolks, then gently fold this mixture into the egg whites.

5 Finally sift in the flour and cocoa mixture with a large metal spoon. Turn into the prepared pan and bake in the oven for 40 minutes.

6 Leave to cool in the cake pan, then turn out, dust with confectioners' sugar and serve.

torta di mandorle

ALMOND CAKE

This simple cake is often served as a teatime treat in my area of Tuscany, although in some households it also graces the table at breakfast time, especially for special occasions. It is traditionally plain, but you could cover it with frosting or fill it with jelly, if you wish.

Makes one 12in cake

1 cup blanched almonds or 1⅓ cups ground almonds
1 teaspoon almond extract
1 cup unsalted butter
4 cups all-purpose flour
1 cup granulated sugar
grated peel of 1 lemon
3 eggs, beaten
3 tablespoons Amaretto liqueur
1 teaspoon cream of tartar
1 teaspoon baking soda
¾ cup warm milk
confectioners' sugar, for dusting

1 Preheat the oven to 325°F. Grind the almonds finely if required, then add the almond extract and mix together.

2 Grease the cake pan thoroughly with some of the butter, then dust with flour.

3 Melt the remaining butter in a small pan and allow it to cool. Sift the remaining flour into a large bowl, stir in the granulated sugar, almonds, and lemon peel.

4 Mix in the eggs, melted butter, and liqueur. Beat the mixture thoroughly. Stir the cream of tartar and the baking soda into the milk, then pour this into the cake mixture and beat again.

5 Pour the cake mixture into the prepared cake pan and bake in the oven for about 1 hour, or until a toothpick inserted into the center of the cake comes out dry and clean. Serve warm or cold, dusted with confectioners' sugar.

torta di mele

ITALIAN APPLE CAKE

This easy cake makes for a very dense result—perfect for picnics or a substantial teatime treat. It is also delicious with pitted and sliced peaches, apricots, or plums. For maximum moisture, I would definitely recommend you use fruit that has plenty of juice, so in the case of apples I would choose ones that are sweet and juicy. You can vary the depth of the baking pan to achieve a different overall texture.

Serves 6 to 8

3 large eggs
¾ cup superfine sugar
2 cups all-purpose flour, sifted
⅔ cup milk
grated peel of ½ lemon
1 heaping teaspoon baking powder, sifted
2 tablespoons butter, cut into small pieces, plus extra for greasing
3 tablespoons stale bread crumbs
6½ cups dessert apples, peeled sliced thin
2 tablespoons granulated or light brown sugar

1 Preheat the oven to 350°F. Beat the eggs in a large bowl until light and fluffy, adding the sugar gradually. Fold in the flour, milk, lemon peel, and baking powder. The mixture should be quite liquid.

2 Grease a 10in cake pan thoroughly with butter, then dust with the bread crumbs. Turn the pan upside down to remove all the loose bread crumbs and discard them.

3 Add half the sliced apples to the cake mixture and stir through. Pour the cake mixture into the pan, arrange the remaining sliced apples on the top, dot with butter, sprinkle with the granulated sugar, and bake in the oven for 55 minutes.

4 Remove from the oven and allow to cool completely before removing from the pan and serving.

torta di riso

ITALIAN RICE CAKE

It is the rich eggy, sticky quality of this cake that makes it so very delicious and incredibly filling! When we were children we used to be given this for tea, because there was a firmly held idea that all the eggs and milk were nourishing and very good for us. I sometimes add crystallized chopped fruit, golden raisins, or nuts to the basic mixture.

Makes one 10in cake

¾ cup short-grain rice
about 5 cups milk
butter, for greasing
2 tablespoons semolina
8 eggs
1¼ cups superfine sugar
3 tablespoons brandy
grated peel of 1 lemon

1 Preheat the oven to 350°F. Place the rice and about two thirds of the milk into a pan and boil for 10 minutes, then drain.

2 Grease a 10in cake pan thoroughly with butter, then sprinkle with the semolina. Do not use a loose-based pan, or all the liquid will ooze away. Turn the cake pan upside down to remove any loose semolina.

3 Beat the eggs in a large bowl until foaming and pale yellow. Add the superfine sugar gradually, beating constantly, then add the brandy and lemon peel.

4 Stir thoroughly, then add the rice and the remaining milk. Pour into the prepared cake pan. Bake in the oven for about 50 minutes, or until a toothpick inserted into the center comes out clean. The cake should be well set and golden brown. Serve warm or cold.

SERVING SUGGESTION ~ This is another really dense, heavy cake, so do serve it in small slices.

torta di zucca

PUMPKIN CAKE

A traditional and delicious recipe from the Veneto region where the humble pumpkin is widely used. The quantities for this cake are calculated in raw weight of pumpkin, so in other words for a cake large enough for four people you will need 1¼lb of pumpkin—double this amount for a larger cake. Choose your cake pan once you have made the cake mixture. If you prefer, you can bake the pumpkin in the oven, then mash it with the butter once it is soft.

Serves 6 to 8

⅔ cup unsalted butter, plus extra for greasing
1¼lb good-quality, ripe, pumpkin, or butternut squash
a pinch of salt
¾ cup granulated sugar
½ cup crushed almonds
⅓ cup candied citron peel
⅓ cup golden raisins, soaked in grappa until swollen
grated peel of 1 lemon
¾ cup all-purpose flour
1 heaping teaspoon baking powder
2 eggs separated
confectioners' sugar, for dusting

1 Preheat the oven to 350°F. Grease and very carefully line a 2in loose-based cake pan.

2 Peel and cube the pumpkin, then place in a saucepan with the butter, and cook until the pumpkin is soft. Remove the pan from the heat, add the salt, and mash thoroughly.

3 Stir in the granulated sugar, almonds, candied citron, golden raisins with the grappa, and the grated lemon peel. Beat together very thoroughly. Sift in the flour and baking powder and stir.

4 Beat the egg yolks in a bowl until light and foamy, then fold into the pumpkin mixture. Beat the egg whites in a separate clean, greasefree bowl until stiff, then fold in lightly.

5 Turn the mixture into the prepared cake pan and bake in the oven for about 1 hour, or until a toothpick inserted into the center of the cake comes out clean.

6 Turn out onto a wire rack to cool and then dust with confectioners' sugar to serve. Please note that this is a very moist cake indeed.

torta margherita

DAISY CAKE

This is the most classic of all the Italian cake recipes. Absolutely simple, very light, and flavored with a faint hint of lemon peel, this cake would be on stand-by for children's teas or for dunking into bowls of milky coffee for breakfast. It is delicious thinly spread with cold jelly that has a slightly tart taste, such as sour plum or cherry. You can also serve it in thin slices to dunk into dessert wine as a very simple finishing touch to your meal.

Makes one 10in cake

butter, for greasing
1½ cups all-purpose flour, sifted, plus extra for dusting
6 eggs, separated
6 tablespoons superfine sugar
¼ cup cornstarch, sifted
1 cup unsalted butter, melted
½ tablespoon grated lemon peel
a pinch of salt
confectioners' sugar, for dusting

1 Preheat the oven to 350°F. Grease a 10in cake pan and dust with flour, tipping out any excess.

2 Beat the egg yolks with the superfine sugar in a large bowl until pale yellow, then gradually beat in the flour and cornstarch.

3 Gradually beat in the melted butter, lemon peel, and salt. Beat the egg whites in a separate greasefree bowl into stiff peaks, then fold into the mixture.

4 Pour the cake mixture into the prepared cake pan and bake in the oven for about 40 minutes, or until a clean knife inserted into the center of the cake comes out completely clean. Leave to cool in the cake pan, then turn out onto a wire rack. Dust with confectioners' sugar to serve.

zabaglione

WHIPPED EGG YOLKS WITH MARSALA

*A*nybody over the age of 35 who has ever been to an Italian
restaurant during the late fifties and throughout the
sixties, seventies, and eighties will have at some time or another
enjoyed this delicious yellow fluffy cloud of a dessert. Requiring
time and energy and dedication to prepare, this remains one of
the most seductive desserts ever created. Sadly, there are fewer
and fewer Italian restaurants that still retain zabaglione on the
menu, opting instead for the ubiquitous tiramisu—which is
more convenient as it can be made well ahead of time! I mourn
the passing of zabaglione and encourage you to rediscover how
wonderful it really is.

❧

Serves 6

6 egg yolks
4 tablespoons cold water
6 tablespoons Marsala
6 tablespoons superfine sugar

1 Place all the ingredients into the top half of a double boiler and beat them all together with a balloon whisk off the heat.

2 Fill the base of the double boiler with hot but not boiling water and place over a low heat.

3 Beat constantly at an even rhythm, always beating in the same direction, and continue for about 20 minutes until the mixture has become light, foamy, and pale yellow. It should be the consistency of semi-melted ice cream. If you undercook it, the liquid will separate from the egg yolks.

4 If the mixture appears to be scrambling, remove it from the heat immediately and beat hard until it is smooth again, holding the top half of the double boiler in a bowl of ice cold water. Never allow the water in the double boiler to actually come to a boil. Serve warm in stemmed glasses.

zuppa inglese

THE ITALIAN VERSION OF THE ENGLISH TRIFLE

*T*his is absolutely nothing like an English trifle, but very delicious nevertheless—I often wonder which came first, the English or the Neapolitan version! What is amusing is that the name, translated literally, means English soup—which has never struck me as being terribly complimentary!

∽

Serves 6

10 tablespoons of your favorite liqueur
10 tablespoons dark rum
2½ cups fresh ricotta cheese
4oz bittersweet baking chocolate
¾ cup granulated sugar
2 teaspoons vanilla extract
2 tablespoons cold water
10oz sponge cake, cut into strips about 2in wide

1 Mix the rum and liqueur in a bowl and pour half into a second bowl. Strain the ricotta into one of the two bowls and mix the alcohol and the ricotta together thoroughly.

2 Grate the chocolate and mix about one third of it into the ricotta mixture.

3 Place the granulated sugar and the vanilla extract in a small pan with the water and melt together until you have a smooth caramel syrup. Allow to cool to hand heat, then pour this into the ricotta mixture gradually, stirring constantly.

4 Dip the sponge cake in the remaining rum and liqueur mixture and arrange a layer in the base of a pretty bowl. Pour over the ricotta mixture, then cover with another layer of dipped cake.

5 Continue until all the cake and the ricotta mixture have been used up, finishing with a layer of ricotta. Cover with the remaining grated chocolate and leave to chill in the refrigerator for 1 hour before serving.

SERVING SUGGESTION ~ You can also make this in individual ramekins or cups. If you wish, you could use mascarpone cheese instead, but the texture is quite different.

Probably the most seductive of all the Italian desserts has to be the gorgeously fluffy, yellow creation that is zabaglione. Those of us who are old enough to have experienced this first hand, will remember what it was like to go for dinner at your local Italian trattoria with a stemmed glass of zabaglione in which to sink a spoon.

This dessert, which contains only three ingredients—sugar, egg yolks, and Marsala wine has to be made just before serving, with patience and dedication. The egg yolks and the wine are blended with the sugar in a bowl, then the bowl is placed over a pan of simmering, steamy water and beaten constantly and steadily until the mixture has become pale yellow and tripled in volume. A good 20 minutes is considered by most to be long enough, undercooking means that it will split and separate into two very different layers, and too much heat or too long a cooking time will give you Marsala-flavored scrambled eggs.

It is a strange juxtaposition of origins. It comes from Piemonte, and there the link with a French season is clear, given that the area used to be part of Savoy. But the use of Marsala, which comes from the town of the same name in Sicily, immediately gives me an insight into that period of Italian history when this very northern mountainous, landlocked region was part of the same Kingdom as the island of Sicily. I am intrigued to know what other recipes and cultural traditions changed hands among cooks during what now seems such an unlikely liaison.

In these days of immediacy, when patience seems low on the list of priorities, at least in the kitchen, the arrival of tiramisu has all but pushed the marvelous zabaglione into a dark and forgotten corner of our memories. Tiramisu can be delicious, and has well and truly taken over the Italian dessert trolley. It is convenient because it can be made in large quantities ahead of time and, in fact improves by being kept for a while. But it somehow lacks the elegance and old-fashioned glamour of the wonderful zabaglione.

Tiramisu has its own origin as a pick me up, which every Italian Mama would prepare for her ailing boy. A blending together of egg yolks and sugar, with mascarpone, a shot of espresso, and a slug of brandy, created a perfect bowl of something sweet and delicious for the dunking of cookies. Italians are mad about dunking and do it very well! From this simple remedy an internationally renowned dessert has been born, which nowadays is created using all kinds of variations, some of them a long way from that original kitchen table.

On the whole, there are very few Italian desserts which can be really and truly classified as classics. After all, in a country that has such wonderful fruit and can boast the best ice cream in the world—they did invent it!—desserts really don't need to play such a significant role.

the italian pantry

TOMATOES

Canned tomatoes: are probably the ultimate canned product
that no Italian pantry can ever be without. Canned tomatoes, or
pelati as they are so fondly known, come in all sorts of varieties
—whole, finely chopped, roughly chopped, and as passata.

Passata: means canned tomatoes that have been sieved into a
thick creamy purée. It is a new development and its main
advantage is that it cooks much more quickly than whole
canned tomatoes, so when you are in a rush to make a really
speedy pasta sauce, this has to be the best choice. I am not a
great fan of canned tomatoes that contain herbs, garlic, or other
flavorings, as to my taste buds the flavoring always seems to
taste sour and somehow not quite true. In any case, I would
always rather add the flavorings I want as I create my dish.

Homemade tomato sauce: Many Italian households also have a
store of homemade tomato sauce, carefully capped tightly in
sterilized bottles, which is the best way to preserve the intensely
fresh taste of real summer tomatoes.

Tomato paste: Concentrated tomato paste, which is used as
sparingly as possible and usually comes in a can or a squeezable
tube, is also an essential part of the tomato section of your pantry.

PASTA

Durum wheat pasta: Dried durum wheat pasta, made under
factory conditions by combining water and flour together,
obviously has to have pride of place next to the tomatoes. After
all, spaghetti and a simple tomato sauce are as natural to every
Italian as breathing! It fascinates me that despite the number of
different shapes available on the market, spaghetti is still the
most popular shape. Every year the various manufacturers

introduce some new shape to their range in an effort to gain larger portions of the market, but the simplicity of spaghetti seems to retain its hold no matter what else is available! Penne, fusilli, maccheroni, farfalle, and conchiglie are almost as popular, but it is also vital, as far as an Italian household is concerned, to have a few packets of small pasta, known as pastina, which are added to soups. Naturally, different regions of Italy also have their own favorites. There are also shapes that have been proven to work best with local traditional sauces and hold a very special place in the kitchens where these amazing combinations of pasta and sauce were first created.

Egg pasta: Dried egg pasta is basically fresh pasta, made with flour and eggs that has been allowed to dry out until it becomes brittle. This pasta definitely tastes quite different from pasta made without egg and is used for more specific recipes, as it is richer and heavier on the digestion.

RICE

Risotto tends to be more popular and far more widely prepared in the north of the country and requires the right kind of rice. It is not possible to achieve the combination of that essential creaminess, surrounding rice grains that are still slightly chewy and al dente, unless you begin with rice that is starchy enough to give you the right end result.

Arborio, Carnaroli and Vialone Nano are three of the best known and most popular varieties, although there are in fact about 15 different types of risotto rice still cultivated across the northern regions.

Arborio: is widely available but has a tendency to overcook.

Carnaroli: has the largest grain and is not so prone to

overcooking. In Italy it is considered to be the best possible rice available and as such is reserved for really very special recipes.
Vialone Nano: with its tiny, very hard grain is the rice best loved by the Venetians and is often used to make risotto containing fish ingredients.

OLIVE OIL

Olive oils vary so much in flavor that I think it is essential to have at least three different bottles on the go at one time in your pantry. There are those that are best suited to being used as a dressing and those that are suitable for cooking. Oils from the south tend to be very intensely flavored and have a heavier quality than those from further north. Olive oil is much less expensive than extra virgin olive oil, although I have to say I prefer to always use extra virgin because I like the fact that it adds a flavor to the dish. Unlike olive oil which is virtually tasteless. In either case, olive oil reaches optimum heat for cooking very quickly and steadily, although it is not very good for browning. If you are looking for a deeper golden brown color, then I would recommend a blend of olive oil or extra virgin olive oil with a seed oil such as sunflower.
Making olive oil: The process of creating olive oil is as old as time itself and despite the introduction of modern machinery that has replaced the ancient methods of turning stones to grind olives, the basic rules remain the same. The olives must be picked from the trees and pressed quickly so that they are as whole and perfect—virginal—as possible. This is because olives that are damaged by bruising or are cracked will begin to decompose and this will spoil the taste of the oil.

At home in Italy our goal was to pick the olives off the tree and bottle as oil within a very short 90 minutes! Olives were never allowed to wait around for any length of time; they were hand-picked, stored, and pressed as fast as possible to capture their freshness.

The pressing: the very first pressing, which constitutes a tiny quantity and is created without any pressure being exerted on the olives, is called *Il fiore*, the flower, and is usually kept by the producer for home use! For the next pressing, a little pressure is applied, and the resulting oil is then checked for oleic acidity level. If the oil shows an acidity level between zero and 1 percent, it is considered qualified for the name extra virgin. The next pressing is slightly more heavy handed and the resulting oil should retain an oleic acidity level of between 1 and 5 percent. This oil is then qualified for virgin olive oil. At this point the olives need to be pressed very hard to extract whatever is left and the result has a much higher oleic acidity level and can only be called olive oil. A final pressing actually grinds the stones of the olives themselves, and the resulting oil, called pomace in England and *sansa* in Italian, is the oil which was used to light the street lamps throughout Italy before the invention of electricity. As a comestible, it is actually corrosive, and should therefore be avoided for cooking and eating purposes at all costs!

VINEGARS

Contrary to what people might think, the use of balsamic vinegar is traditionally really much more limited in Italy than its popularity outside of the country might lead one to suppose. Good-quality vinegars made with either red or white wine are much more generally used in areas that are not within the production areas of Emilia Romagna, and specifically the provinces of Modena and Reggio Emilia. Real balsamic vinegar is a condiment that has very old origins and to this day is produced privately, at home, in the attics of the grand old houses of Modena and Reggio Emilia. It is the men of the household who prepare the balsamic vinegar, using barrels of various sizes. When their daughters marry, the bride takes a proportion of the father's balsamic with her as part of her dowry, thus ensuring that the family tradition is kept going from one generation to the next.

Making balsamic vinegar: the barrels are made of different woods, all of which are coopered from trees that grow only within the confines of the province and that have a perfume and flavor of their own, which they add to the vinegar during the long process of maturation. Boiled wine must (grape juice, which is just beginning to ferment) is the basic ingredient. The boiled wine is allowed to mature in the open top barrels, with small quantities being poured from one barrel into another in order to absorb as much of the flavors imparted by the wood's resins as possible and mix each batch of balsamic with the next creating a completely unique taste. This balsamic, which is hard to call vinegar, needs at least 12 years of aging to create the right balance and it may be aged for considerably longer. The end result is thick and sticky, quite unlike the more liquid version of the product that is prepared commercially under stringent factory conditions.

CAPERS, ANCHOVIES, AND OLIVES

These three ingredients, more than any others, typify for me the strong flavors that are identifiable as an essential part of the cuisine of the southern regions. There is something quite harsh about these particular flavors, which come from the heat of the sun beating down on soil that has become parched and cracked from lack of rainfall.

Capers: grow from a marvelously succulent plant that produces glorious flowers. It is a plant that is nothing short of miraculous in terms of its ability to find a fissure in a wall or pile of stones to anchor its roots.

Anchovies: the silver anchovy, once so plentiful in the waters surrounding the peninsula and the islands of Italy that as a child I could catch a hundred of them simply by scooping my bucket through the water, is preserved in sea salt to add a salty, surprising non-fishy taste to all kinds of dishes from sauces for pasta to roast lamb. They are popular in the north of the country too, in particular in landlocked Piemonte, where finding fresh fish used to be too challenging a prospect and thus the evolution of dishes using preserved fish has taken place over time.

Olives: Table olives are a much bigger industry than olive oil and literally come in all shapes and sizes and variations of color. Whole, chopped, or puréed, they add an unmistakable blend of flavors to all kinds of dishes.

DRIED CHILES—PEPERONCINO

Dried red chiles are vital for the preparation of many dishes that are unmistakably southern; in particular the region of Basilicata excels in the preparation of dishes using the spice that they call *Il diavolicchio*, the little devil.

HERBS

Basil: is the herb of Liguria, where pesto comes from, and for me is the most instant flavor of summertime.

Rosemary: is the taste of Tuscany and fills my senses with the flavor of home.

Sage: is allowed to infuse melted butter to make a classic pasta

condiment simply called *burro e salvia* (butter and sage).
Oregano: is the only herb worth using in a dried form and in
fact is improved immeasurably by drying.
Parsley: the most vital herb for cooking classically, like an
Italian, is flat-leaf or Italian parsley, which needs to be kept
fresh in your kitchen like a bunch of flowers, used for color and
flavor in literally hundreds of different savory dishes.

GARLIC AND ONIONS

There is a strongly held conviction among many people that
Italian food is laden with garlic. This is a bit of an exaggeration
and is definitely a generalization. Some Italian dishes are very
heavy on garlic, but the majority of Italian recipes call for garlic
to be used subtly. It is the onion that is more important with
many different varieties used—red and sweet, white and mild,
or strong and brown. The gentle frying together of garlic, onion
or a combination of onion, carrot, and celery is called a *soffritto*,
and is the traditional way in which many, not to say most Italian
recipes begin.

conversion charts

Use this basic guide for converting measurements from cup and imperial measures to metric. Volumes are standard. Weight can vary according to the density of the ingredients, so the basic ingredients should be used as a rough guide.

USING CUP AND SPOON MEASURES	
All cup and spoon measures should be level (unless otherwise stated).	
¼ teaspoon	1.25ml
½ teaspoon	2.5ml
1 teaspoon	5ml
1 tablespoon	15ml

LIQUID MEASURES		
Cup	**Imperial**	**Metric**
¼ cup	2fl oz	60ml
1 cup	8fl oz	250ml
1¼ cups	½ pint	300ml
1½ cups	12fl oz	350ml
1¾ cups	14fl oz	400ml
2 cups	16fl oz	475ml
2½ cups	1 pint	600ml
3 cups	1¼ pints	750ml
4 cups	1¾ pints	1 liter

WEIGHTS			
Imperial	**Metric**	**Imperial**	**Metric**
¼lb	100g	1lb 2oz	500g
6oz	175g	1¼lb	575g
½lb	225g	1½lb	675g
12oz	350g	1¾lb	800g
1lb	450g	2¼lb	1kg

OVEN TEMPERATURES

°F	°C	Gas
225	110	¼
250	120	½
275	140	1
300	150	2
325	160	3
350	180	4
375	190	5
400	200	6
425	220	7
450	230	8
475	250	9

BASIC INGREDIENTS
Cup and Weight Equivalents

Bread crumbs, dry	1 cup = 2½oz / 65g
Bread crumbs, fresh	1 cup = 2oz / 50g
Butter	1 cup = 8oz / 225g 2 tablespoons = 2oz / 50g
Cheese, grated Cheddar	1 cup = 4oz / 100g
Confectioners' (icing) sugar	1 cup = 4oz / 100g
Cornstarch (cornflour)	1 cup = 8oz / 225g
Cream cheese, ricotta	1 cup = 8oz / 225g
Flour	1 cup = 4oz / 100g
Honey	1 cup = 8oz / 225g
Parmesan cheese, grated	1 cup = 3oz / 75g
Peas, frozen	1 cup = 4oz / 100g
Polenta	1 cup = 5oz / 150g
Rice, long grain types	1 cup = 7oz / 200g
Sugar, granulated or superfine	1 cup (generous) = 8oz / 225g 1 cup (scant) = 7oz / 200g

INDEX

Entries in *italics* refer to recipe names

Valentina wrote her first book, *Perfect Pasta,* in 1984 and has since gone on to publish more than 20 books. Although better known for her link with Italy and Italian food culture, she was originally trained in classical French cuisine. Valentina's original BBC television series *Italian Regional Cookery* was shown in 1990 and 1998 to international acclaim. She is the founder and director of Villa Valentina Cookery Holidays Ltd. and has been conducting and teaching cookery classes for over 10 years, alongside her ongoing career as a celebrity chef, author, broadcaster, and lecturer.